The Kimberley
AUSTRALIA'S WILD OUTBACK WILDERNESS

"This ravine, in the luxuriance of its vegetation, and the great size of the trees, as well as in its rapid stream, at times leaping in cascades, or foaming in rapids, resembled those we had before seen in the sandstone ranges, but it differed from them in the height of the surrounding hills and cliffs, which being overshadowed with hanging trees and climbing plants, presented as rich a painting as the eye could behold: and as these grew golden with the rays of the setting sun, or were thrown into deep and massive shadows, I could not but regret that no Claude of the tropics had arisen to transfer to canvass scenes which words cannot express."[1]

"To ascend a hill and say you are the first civilised man who has ever trod this spot… to descry new mountains, to dart your eager glance down unexplored valleys and unvisited glens…to trace the course of rivers which tempt you onward to the bosom of unknown lands. These are the joys of an explorer's life!"[2]

Hugh Brown   www.hughbrown.com

Dedication

To Joy, Nathan and Adam, Ali and your extended families who have provided such support and friendship over the last thirteen years. You mean an incredible amount to me.

And to "Tank", whose inspiration, memory and example, live with me every day.

The Kimberley
Australia's Wild Outback Wilderness

ISBN 0 9752054 0 4

March 2004

Hugh Brown
PO Box 1918
BROOME WA 6725
Telephone: +61 418 936 517

Disclaimer

While every effort has been made to ensure its accuracy, the information contained in this book has been included as a guide only and not as a basis for the making of decisions that will vary according to individual needs. Weather and road conditions can change suddenly and people should make their own checks prior to travelling into what are, in many cases, remote areas. People should ensure they have an adequate supply of food, water and spare tyres to sustain them for up to a week in the event of mechanical breakdown. When walking, people should consume at least one litre of water per hour to avoid dehydration.

Table of Contents

Title Page	1
Dedication	2
Disclaimer	2
A. Acknowledgements	7
B. Foreword	8
C. Introduction	9
D. Kimberley Map	10
H. Broome and the Dampier Peninsula	12
1. Broome	12
2. Camels on/and Cable Beach	15
3. Roebuck Bay	18
4. Gantheaume Point	22
5. Riddell Beach	24
6. Cape Leveque	26
F. The Kimberley Coast	30
1. Introduction	30
2. Pearling and the Kimberley coast	38
3. Kimberley Tides	46
4. King George Falls	50
5. King Cascade	53
6. Horizontal Waterfall	56
7. Buccaneer Archipelago	58

- G. Derby and the Gibb River Road 66
  1. Introduction 66
  2. Cattle 70
  3. El Questro Wilderness Park 76
  4. Kalumburu 78
  5. Mitchell Falls 80
  6. Bradshaw Rock-art 82
  7. The Spirit Wandjina 84
  8. The Charnley River 86
  9. Manning Gorge 88
  10. Bell Gorge 90
  11. Lennard River Gorge 92
  12. Boab Trees 94
  13. Derby 100
  14. King Sound 102
- H. Fitzroy Crossing and the Devonian Reef National Parks 104
  1. Introduction 104
  2. Windjana Gorge 106
  3. Tunnel Creek 108
  4. Build-up Boab – Blina Station, Great Northern Highway 110
  5. Geikie Gorge 112
  6. Fitzroy Crossing 116
- I. Halls Creek and Surrounds 118
  1. Halls Creek 118

2. Wolfe Creek Crater 120
3. Shadow Detail: Osmond Range 124
4. Lake Gregory 125
5. Albert Edward Range 126
6. Palm Springs 128
7. Saw Tooth Gorge 130
8. China Wall 132
9. Barramundi Fishing 133
10. Purnululu National Park 134

- J. Kununurra/Wyndham 142
    1. Kununurra 142
    2. Lily Creek, Lake Kununurra and Sleeping Buddha 144
    3. Black Rock Falls 146
    4. Electrical Storm 148
    5. Wyndham 150
    6. Crocodiles 154
    7. Ivanhoe Crossing 158
    8. Lake Argyle 160
    9. Revolver Creek Falls 164
    10. Cockburn Range 166
    11. Ragged Range 170
    12. Argyle Diamond Mine 172

- BIBLIOGRAPHY 174
- FOOTNOTES 177

A word from the photographer about the equipment used

Most of the photographs shown here have been shot using Canon EOS1N cameras with three lenses: EF 16-35mm f2.8 L USM; EF 50mm f2.5; and, EF 70-200mm f2.8 L IS USM. Hugh does not believe in the artificial enhancement of images through the use of filters. The majority of the images included in this book have been shot using Fuji Velvia 50 transparency (slide) film rated at 40, though in recent times Hugh has been impressed with the results provided by Kodak's E100VS transparency film: particularly for aerial work. Hugh relies on Churchill Colour Laboratories in Leederville for all film and processing needs. Their quality and service is unparalleled in Western Australia. For his Limited Edition Photographic prints, Hugh relies exclusively on Ilfochrome archival photographic paper (no other photographic paper comes close to offering the same colour gamut and finish) and the wonderful work of the Created for Life Print Lab at Erina (north of Sydney).

Acknowledgements

This book is the result of six years of living, travelling, enjoying and suffering throughout the Kimberley. Many of these photographs would never have been possible without the encouragement and assistance of the following people:

- If not for the encouragement of Jo Armstrong (Always Printing Ideas) I would never have entered the realms of professional photography. Likewise, Philip Quirk and the team at the Wildlight Photo Agency have been a major force behind my photographic development and are owed a great deal of gratitude.

- Thank you to Dave and Dipper for your kind words and friendship and to Simon ("Booster") Thorpe, and his family, Liz, Ali and Riley, for accommodating me and assisting me to gain access to many of the photos you see here. I look forward to many more trips out bush.

- Peter Wieland and his staff at Alligator Airways, put me in the position to capture many of the aerial photographs that you see here. It would be hard to find a group of more professional pilots.

- Marie, Susan and Rachel at the Kimberley Bookshop, were perhaps my major sounding board for the entire project and without their encouragement, support and insight, this book may never have been published.

- Over the last twelve months, I worked closely with the team at Kailis Australian Pearls. Many of these photos are the result of that collaboration. To Janelle, Kylie and everyone else involved, thank you.

- Russell Gueho and his partner, Vanessa Hayden, have been great friends during my time in the Kimberley and Russell is one of the most knowledgeable people on the Kimberley that I know. Both provided much critical input into what you now read. Likewise, Tim Willing, Ali Spencer and Ali and David ("SS") Pentelow reviewed numerous versions of the final draft and helped me to isolate factual inaccuracies. All have been amazing in their willingness to share knowledge and time.

- Brian Smallwood and the team at ARB 4 x 4 Accessories, together with Stewart Macdonald of Vertical Events and Ian Huxley and the Westshore Group (proprietors of the Sand Bar and Grill) have been strong and encouraging supporters and I look forward to being able to repay their faith.

- Thanks are also owed to Allen Grosse and CALM, for providing me with access to their excellent library, Steve ("Mudlark") Madden, Ian ("Nigel") Obern, Les Russ, Fred Russ, Laurence Birch, Viv McMicking of the Wyndham Historical Society, Charlie Sharpe of Lake Argyle Cruises, Chris Kloss, Kevin Shaw, "JR" and "Killer" at the Bureau of Meteorology, Kim Epton, Cathie Clement, Martin Van Kranendonk of the WA Geological Survey and the Water and Rivers Commission in Kununurra.

- Greg Taylor at *TM Typographics,* put in so many hours of his time to making this project what it has now become. His design skills and knowledge of the printing industry have proven absolutely first rate. He can be contacted on 08 9474 2610.

Foreword

It is with great pleasure that I provide this Foreword to what is an outstanding publication by Hugh Brown. We have been great friends for almost fifteen years when we studied in Geelong together. He has become a part of many families, including mine, with his unique and insightful wit and charm. He always gave the impression that there needed to be more in his life than work and study, despite his brilliant intellect. In moving from Melbourne to remote Western Australia he discovered the passions that he has combined in this publication - photography and the Australian outback.

We are all familiar with the old cliché that a picture paints a thousand words. The landscapes in this publication are evidence of that. But beyond the pictures, Hugh's words in this book put the images into context giving the reader a tremendous insight behind the beauty. And that has become the common thread behind his work. He has come to know and love the land he has represented in this book - and to me it sets it apart. It is not a compilation of tourist snaps, it is a collection of images carefully captured and explained that provide understanding and evoke a desire to visit first-hand.

I am sure this publication will be the first of several.

David Matthews

I am also pleased to be contributing to this book. I first met Hughy on a trip through a remote Arnhem land community - Oenpelli - in 2000. We trekked through the ranges, swam at the Number One waterfall and got to know the community. He left an immediate impression with his commentary on the life and the landscape of remote Australia. And he travelled light ! One backpack, one fishing rod, a change of clothes and of course his trusty camera. This publication is the result of much hard work and dedication and I congratulate him on the result. I must also add that the man barracks for Hawthorn, so I can safely say that Hugh, having enjoyed the 80's more than most, was happy to move from Melbourne safe in the knowledge he had seen five premierships and two Brownlow Medals (won by John Platten and some other bloke). Well done Hughy !

Robert Dipierdomenico

Introduction

I first travelled to the Kimberley in 1998 while on vacation. Within six months I was living here, and I have remained here, with the exception of a short break, ever since. People say that there is something magic about the Kimberley: something that keeps drawing one back. For me, that magic is many things. Deep rivers and gorges, forged over millions of years, redefine our concept of beauty and challenge our sense of place. Thunderstorms ignite lightning shows with the branches of a thousand laser beams and electrify dark foreboding skies. Channels of flood-swollen creeks move with the rush of a thousand horses. And the taste of home-made rum and vodka, beneath a billion stars, washes away our meaningless pressures of time. The Kimberley ignites our emotions like few other places on earth.

Even in the difficult times out bush – and there have been far too many to recount here – there is something special in the feeling of euphoria that only an untouched magical wilderness can deliver. The Kimberley is a place of paradoxes. Spectacular ranges, escarpments, gorges and what must surely be amongst the most stunning coastlines on earth, mask many hidden dangers. Recently, a walk along the King Edward River in the north Kimberley was compromised by the presence of numerous large, pointy-horned, irritable scrub short-horn bulls. This, as I walked along a black-soil plain characterised by thick 3-metre-high spear-grass and an absence of trees. Even as I write this piece, my desire to go swimming with some 2 metre Lemon Sharks is tempered by the knowledge that a 4 metre saltwater crocodile was sighted around the corner from the bay in which I now sit, only days ago.

This is the first of several books that I hope to produce on the Kimberley. It is intentionally short and directed at covering the popular spots to which many visitors go when they come here. I have avoided exposing some of the "secret" places known only to the locals. There are enough places to occupy many months of travelling here without risking the sanctity and fragility of what is a precious wilderness. It will be a major challenge over the next 50 to 100 years to manage increased visitation and the desire of Governments to grow our small Kimberley population. My hope is that this precious wilderness will also be a lasting one.

Throughout the text, I have frequently used the word "discovered". This is not intended to diminish the habitation of Aboriginal peoples. It refers to the more recent identification and naming of the places covered by our early European explorers.

And one final word for those seeking to gain further insight into the Kimberley and its history, geology and natural history. Russell Gueho has recently published an excellent book that conveys much of the learnings he gained while working as a wildlife officer across the Kimberley over many years. It is entitled **Icons of the Kimberley.**

D Kimberley Map

Sunset in the Buccaneer Archipelago

Book Narrative - **Kimberley Map**

11

E Broome and the Dampier Peninsula

1. Broome

While current day Derby can be considered a product of its century-old pastoral roots, Broome was a town that was founded, and grew, on pearling.

Broome, like Derby, was gazetted as a townsite on 27 November 1883. However, it was not until after the cyclone of 1887, when more than 140 people died and 22 vessels were lost, that its visible development as a townsite became apparent. It was recognised that the north-west pearling fleet needed a servicing and supply-base and a base from which to repair severely damaged vessels. Prior to that, and frustrated by its lack of "progress", its namesake, Sir Frederick Napier Broome, had written:

I believe the township named after me by the Hon. Surveyor General is likely to remain a mere 'dummy' townsite, inhabited by the tenants of three graves...My present idea is to have the name cancelled.[3]

Not only did pearling provide the foundation and impetus for Broome's future growth, but it also acted as the stimulant for the influx of the many different nationalities that characterise Broome's present population. Toward the end of the Nineteenth Century Broome was a town of social and class hierarchies: not unlike many other areas of Australia. Pearling – with its high mortality rate and poor pay and living conditions – was an industry that struggled to attract white Australians. Instead, it relied on the industry and courage of the many willing Malays, Chinese, Japanese and Aboriginal peoples for whom the poor pay and living conditions compared well with what they would have received at home and/or elsewhere. Often though, the Aboriginal participants were not willing.[4]

Today, Broome is a thriving, modern economy incorporating many of the trappings that might once have been considered the exclusive domain of the larger population centres. Pearling remains an important industry though the town is now also endowed with a thriving property market (Broome Real Estate reports capital growth rates in excess of 20% per annum) and a burgeoning tourism industry. Further prospects exist for Broome to develop as a major servicing and supply-base to the nearby oil and gas fields of the Browse Basin.

This photograph was taken of the Shinju Matsuri Festival in Chinatown. Held in August each year, the Festival celebrates Broome's multiculturalism and pearling heritage.

Broome and the Dampier Peninsula - **Broome**

Broome

Chinatown is Broome's main shopping district and is located near the top of Dampier Creek. For those seeking proximity to Chinatown and its many pearling outlets, Moonlight Bay Apartments is within walking distance and offers stunning views of Roebuck Bay.

2. Camels on/and Cable Beach

The unusual white sand of Cable Beach is thought to overlay a plain of red pindan sandstone with the covering being not more than 3 metres thick. This red sandstone terminates in other areas around Broome as vertical cliffs fronted by narrow high-tide beaches (eg, Riddell Beach and Gantheaume Point).

Eventually, it is predicted, the white sands of Cable Beach will disappear: though not in the next 100 years. Each Dry season prevailing south-easterly winds combine with westerly currents to drive sand from Cable Beach. This process is not reversed during the wet when south-westerly currents and westerly winds drive sand north and inland (from the beach) respectively. The existence of exposed dune cores suggests that replacement sand is not being deposited onto the beach and that whatever sand supply existed previously has been exhausted. Willie Creek is a "sediment sink" and traps sand that has come from Cable Beach and stops sand that has come from north from moving further south toward Cable Beach.[5]

Growing in the shelter of Cable Beach's dunes are a number of isolated pockets of open, deciduous vine thickets. These vine thickets are thought by some to represent the most southerly habitat for vine thickets on Australia's west coast. Related to Queensland's coastal rainforests they contain plants with "ancient Gondwanan affinities: linking in to the now dispersed floras of India, Madagascar, Africa and South America".[6]

Camels were introduced to the Kimberley during the Halls Creek gold-rush of 1886, when they were used to transport supplies from Derby. They were also used extensively in the construction of the Canning Stock Route. The first camels are thought to have been released into Western Australia in the early 1870s by one or more of the Gosse, Warburton and Giles expeditions. Until 1897, when importation was banned due to intense lobbying from operators of traditional horse teams (affected by reduced cartage rates), some 7,000 – 10,000 camels are estimated to have been brought into Western Australia from South Australia and overseas.

Camels on/and Cable Beach

Cable Beach extends for 22 kilometres from Gantheaume Point to Willie Creek. It takes its name from the undersea telegraph line that once linked Australia with London and came ashore at Station Hill overlooking Cable Beach.

Broome and the Dampier Peninsula - **Camels on/and Cable Beach**

3. Roebuck Bay

Captain Philip Parker King named Roebuck Bay in 1819 after the vessel used by William Dampier in his 1699 voyage along the Western Australian coast (though historians now suggest that Dampier landed at Lagrange Bay at the northern end of the Eighty Mile Beach and not at Roebuck Bay).[7]

Roebuck Bay is significant, not only for its natural beauty and diversity of marine life, but also for the fact that it forms a key destination in the annual migration of the Siberian wader-birds. The annual round-trip approximates 30,000 kilometres and it is estimated that 850,000 birds make the journey south seeking coastal tidal flats fertile with food. They arrive in October and November and stay for 6 – 7 months. By the time of their departure, somewhere between March and May, they will have increased their body-weight by 30 – 40%. Though the breeding season in the Siberian Arctic is relatively short, what makes this annual cycle even more remarkable is the change in temperatures that they must endure: from the humidity and 40 degree-plus temperatures of the Kimberley to the sub-zero climate of the Siberian Arctic.

Like elsewhere in the Kimberley, weather has played a huge part in fostering the rich marine-life that so characterises Roebuck Bay, and an analysis of Kimberley weather statistics is an interesting exercise in its own right. The highest *recorded* maximum temperature was 47.9^0 Celsius ("C") at Fitzroy Crossing on 1 January 1969. The lowest recorded maximum temperature was 11.3^0C at Halls Creek on 2 July 1938. The highest minimum temperature was 33.5^0C at Cadjeput (near Fitzroy Crossing) on 1 March 1998 and the lowest recorded minimum temperature was -1.3^0C at Mt Elizabeth Station (on the Gibb River Road) on 26 June 1998. The highest recorded rainfall in a 24 hour period was 635mm at Kilto Station – to the north-east of Broome – on 5 December 1970. The highest monthly rainfall was 1321.7mm at Roebuck Plains Station in January 1917.[8]

Roebuck Bay is perhaps Australia's most important Siberian Wader-bird habitat. This stems from its unique combination of food-rich mangrove mudflats, sheltered high-tide roosts and sandy tidal flats; all within close proximity of each other (important given their considerable energy requirements after their long journey).[9]

Broome and the Dampier Peninsula - **Roebuck Bay**

Writing during his 1892 residence at Marigui, in the St George Basin on the north-west Kimberley coast, pioneer pastoralist, Aeneas Gunn noted:

"The storm was one of the primal, elemental passions of nature. Its power and might and majesty were awe-inspiring, unimaginable and indescribable, but one of us, at least, has the interpretation of Wagner in his heart…The Kokk-i-bob inaugurated the wet season. It was Nature's overture to her grand opera, the north-west monsoons, which had been advertised largely on sky and air, hill and valley for some weeks previously. Almost every evening we were treated to magnificent displays of electrical fireworks, accompanied by great winds, heavy rains and fanfaronades of thunder".[10]

Broome and the Dampier Peninsula - **Roebuck Bay**

Gantheaume Point was originally, but erroneously, named Gantheaume Island by Nicolas Baudin during his 1803 voyage in the Geographe.[11] It was later corrected to its current name by Captain Philip Parker King in his 1821 voyage along the Kimberley coast in the Bathurst.[12] On the northern side of the Point, Anastasia's Pool was built during the 1920s by the then lighthouse keeper for his arthritic wife. Some 500 metres off-shore from Gantheaume Point is an 80 metre deep shore-parallel trough. This "gorge" was created during the last Ice Age about 30,000 years ago when the sea level dropped to minus 100 metres. It contrasts with the shallower Cable Beach seabed that slopes gently to a wide flat plain of 10 – 14 metres in depth.[13]

Broome and the Dampier Peninsula - **Gantheaume Point**

5. Riddell Beach

The pindan (or earthy red) colour that characterises many of the soils and sands around Broome, including Roebuck Bay, is largely a function of their iron oxide coating. At Riddell Beach, sand grains have been bridged by clays and iron oxides. When wet, pindan clays become soft and greasy and erode rapidly, forming steep, deep-sided gullies.[14]

Broome and the Dampier Peninsula - Riddell Beach

6. Cape Leveque

Comprised of sandstones deposited by tidal currents in shallow seas 135 million years ago, the stunning red cliffs of Cape Leveque were first recorded by Europeans during William Dampier's voyage of 1688. They were named after Pierre Leveque, the hydrographer who accompanied French navigator Nicolas Baudin in his voyage along the Western Australian coast in 1803.

The waters off Cape Leveque form part of the annual migratory journey of the Humpback Whale that comes to the Kimberley coast to breed from the cold southern waters of Antarctica. The Humpback cow gives birth to a single calf, weighing up to 2 tonnes, after a gestation period of 11 months. They are known to travel as far as the King George River in the north Kimberley. The breeding season generally takes place between August and September when the waters off the Kimberley coast are around 27^0C. After a fattening period of 2 – 4 weeks, the mothers and newborn calves commence their southern migration with the rest of the pod. During this time, the calves will consume between 200 and 400 litres of their mother's milk daily. The elaborate sounds of the Humpback may reflect one or more of a number of intentions, including the desire to mate, and the portrayal of stamina, experience and power.

The area around Cape Leveque was most probably engulfed by a massive tsunami (tidal wave) as recently as 300 years ago that flooded nearby Leveque Island and then the Cape itself. This event is thought to have been responsible for the unusual porcelainite blocks that lie atop the sandstone cliffs, some 60 metres above sea-level, on the western side of the Cape, and the flat pavement-like rocks that line the cliffs' base.

In recent years there has been a push to upgrade the 201 kilometre red pindan-sand road to at least "all-weather" standard. While there is no question that it is one of the worst major roads in the Kimberley, it is this factor that has thus far controlled access and limited the environmental damage that so often comes with increased visitation. The development and implementation of a carefully thought-out tourism and vehicular management strategy is essential before the road is upgraded to ensure protection of what is a very fragile environment.

This scene, captured during the middle of the wet season, is one of the more beautiful that I have witnessed during my time in the Kimberley. It was taken after a short swim and passing rain shower.

Broome and the Dampier Peninsula - **Cape Leveque**

Cape Leveque

Cape Leveque is today the subject of a low-key tourism development. After the automation of the lighthouse in 1986, the area was purchased by the Aboriginal Development Commission and a number of other Government agencies for the local Djarindjin and One Arm Point Aboriginal communities.

Broome and the Dampier Peninsula - **Cape Leveque**

F. The Kimberley Coast

1. Introduction

I first travelled the Kimberley coast in May 2000 and was immediately struck by its purity, grandeur and beauty. It must surely be one of the few places on earth where humankind has had only limited or, some might argue, negligible impact.

The earliest recorded European visit to the Kimberley coast was in 1644 by Abel Tasman. While his log has since been lost and it is not known exactly where he landed, subsequent narratives of his trip (eg, Thevenot 1663) show that he explored the north coast from Arnhem Land to Exmouth Gulf (appearing to have landed at Roebuck Bay at the very least).[15]

William Dampier, it appears, landed on either the Dampier Peninsula (north of Broome) or Joseph Bonaparte Gulf (to the east of Cambridge Gulf in the north-east Kimberley) in 1688[16] and then at Lagrange Bay in 1699[17]. Nicolas Baudin followed on his 1803 voyage in the *Naturaliste* and discovered and named, *inter alia*, the Bonaparte Archipelago, the Lacepede Islands, Cape Leveque, Gantheaume Island (later corrected to Gantheaume Point by King) and Cape Domet at the eastern head of Cambridge Gulf.[18]

Between 1818 and 1822 Captain Philip Parker King explored and charted much of the Kimberley coast, discovering and naming such icons as, *inter alia*, Mt Trafalgar and Mt Waterloo, the Buccaneer Archipelago, and the rivers, Prince Regent, Hunter and Roe. He is regarded by some as the greatest of Australia's maritime explorers.

King was followed by Lieutenant George Grey (later to become Governor of South Australia) in the wet season of 1837. Grey ventured as far north as Hanover Bay and Port George IV and explored much of the country between the Prince Regent River and the Glenelg River. It was largely as a result of Grey's observations that unscrupulous Victorian promoters initiated the establishment of the Kimberley's disastrous first settlement at Camden Harbour in 1864. Grey was met at Port George IV by Captain Wickham and John Lort Stokes who, in their vessel, the *Beagle*, had surveyed much of the coast from the Dampier Peninsula and King Sound; discovering and naming the Fitzroy River en route.

The Kimberley coast truly is a special place and one that must quickly be protected, in its entirety[19], as a National Park. From the water, it is a place of rugged sandstone cliffs, gorges and escarpment, terraced sandstone islands, white silica beaches, ancient Aboriginal midden mounds, rock paintings and burial sites and violent tidal currents. It is a place of bountiful marine and animal life, boiling with fish, dugong, dolphins, sharks and turtles. And from the air, it is a place of patterns, mosaic-like islands, hidden bays and inlets, and winding snake-like tidal creeks and rivers.

The Kimberley Coast - **Introduction**

A Livistona Palm stands atop an outcrop of glowing sandstone on Palm Island in the Bonaparte Archipelago. This island is unusual among neighbouring islands for its quantity of Livistona Palms. Like many of the islands in the north Kimberley, it is characterised by highly dissected terraced sandstone covered by thick spinifex. It took two of us two hours to gain 200 metres in elevation carrying swags, an esky, a bucket of oysters and camera gear.

Introduction

The Kimberley is home to seventeen species of mangroves. Coastal species use a variety of means to survive extended saltwater immersion. Some root systems are able to store air bubbles, while others excrete salt. Mangrove communities play a vital role in coastline stabilisation by colonising newly created prograding shorelines.[20] They also slow water movement which enables suspended sediments to fall out of suspension and the biological material that they provide breaks down and becomes a primary feed source for fish, molluscs and crustaceans.[21] Aboriginal peoples once ground bark of the freshwater mangrove for addition to water as a fish poison and chewed its leaves to act as a local anaesthetic for afflictions such as tooth-ache. This photograph was taken in the Bonaparte Archipelago on the north-west Kimberley coast.

The Kimberley Coast - **Introduction**

Introduction

Known as "Nigel" for its resemblance to the head of an Aboriginal man. This boulder is the result of intense wind and water erosion along a one-time joint or fracture. Sand-based layers are more resistant than clay-based layers and erode more slowly. A major factor in jointing in the Kimberley is the dry season temperature variances: from near zero in some areas at night to the mid thirties during the day. As rock expands and contracts, large forces are created and it is not uncommon for large explosions to occur; particularly at night-time.

Sunrise in the Bonaparte Archipelago. On the evening before, we had set a fire on this beach and enjoyed a feed of hand-sized oysters and some of the finest table-fish imaginable: Mangrove Jack, Green Snapper and Coral Trout. I find it a shame these days that so many people are losing touch with our natural environment – and its importance to humankind. Ultimately, this can only lead to the destruction of the riches upon which we rely for our continued sustenance.

The Kimberley Coast - **Introduction**

Unusual early August morning cloud build-up covers the North Kimberley sky in the vicinity of Swift Bay. The cloud was a precursor to out-of-season morning rain on a number of days later that week.

The Kimberley Coast - **Introduction**

2. Pearling and the Kimberley Coast

Though the Kimberley region is one of the most sparsely populated regions on earth for its geographical location, it is this very factor that has enabled the Kimberley coast to become internationally regarded for the quality of its Australian South Sea pearls: among the most prized on earth. Crystal clear, pristine waters, teaming with marine life, combine to offer the perfect habitat for the nurturing and growth of pearls that will ultimately be judged according to their colour, shape, size, blemishes and lustre.

Early development of the Kimberley pearling industry was predicated largely on the exploitation of Mother of Pearl shell rather than the pearl itself, although Mother of Pearl shell would appear to have been widely traded by local Aboriginal peoples and used as an item in ceremonies for millennia previously. Aboriginal peoples are said to have used it in rain-making ceremonies and to cover parts of the body, as ornamentation and as a cure for a variety of illnesses. Incised pearl shell, traded between neighbouring groups, is said to have found its way as far south as South Australia, although Aboriginal people are thought to have had little regard for the pearl itself[22], one of which would be found in every 5,000 shells.[23]

The first recorded European acknowledgement of the commercial potential of Pinctada Maxima was by William Dampier at Shark Bay during his 1699 voyage in the *Roebuck*. However, it was not until 1861, when Francis Gregory discovered large quantities along the Pilbara coast at the head of Nickol Bay, that an industry was launched. Within a short time, a lucrative trade for buttons and ornaments had developed to such an extent that the Pilbara grounds had become over fished and Broome had taken over as the centre for pearling in Western Australia. In 1880, Broome is said to have been home to over 400 pearl luggers and more than 3,500 people fishing for pearl shell.[24]

Early day pearling effused little of the romance with which we view it today. Divers battled daily the threats posed by crocodiles, sharks, sea-snakes, manta rays, gropers, blood poisoning, drowning, scurvy or coral fouling their lifelines. Between 1887 and 1935, at least 530 lives and at least 72 vessels had been lost to cyclones that had crossed the Kimberley coast between the Eighty Mile Beach (then called the Ninety Mile Beach) and Beagle Bay. And between 1909 and 1917, at least 145 deaths had been attributed to the bends or divers paralysis brought about by the introduction of hard hat diving and the accompanying use of hand, and later mechanical, air pumps.[25]

A beautiful Kailis Australian South Sea Pearl. Australia's South Sea pearls are found in the silver lipped Pinctada Maxima (or the Mother of Pearl shell oyster as it is otherwise known) and generally fall within a size range of 10mm – 16mm: though smaller and larger pearls are not infrequently found. They are created when an irritant finds its way into the pearl shell causing the oyster to coat the irritant with layers of nacre when the object cannot be expelled. It is these layers of nacre that give the pearl its unique iridescence.

The Kimberley Coast - **Pearling**

Pearling and the Kimberley Coast

Japanese pearling technician Sato evaluates another beautiful Kailis Australian South Sea Pearl. Most technicians are still Japanese, although more Australians are entering the profession annually. The best technicians are highly skilled and can be worth up to A$1M more annually to the company engaging them than the lesser performers. To become accredited as a technician, one must undergo a gruelling five-year training process. After completing the Australian season, many technicians travel overseas to locations elsewhere in the Asia Pacific.

The Kimberley Coast - **Pearling**

Today's pearling industry is very different to the one that faced our early pioneers. Hard hats have been replaced by long lines, and luggers by mother ships and float planes. As a general rule today, and depending upon the tides, divers, at the beginning of the year, dive to collect wild shell which is taken to a designated area where it will be cleaned and rested prior to seeding in June or July. At seeding time, the shell is brought aboard the operating vessel where it is prised open by a wooden clamp. An incision is made from the gonad, and a bead and piece of mantle tissue from another oyster are inserted. These will provide the cells that will form the pearl sac and secrete the pearly nacre around the nucleus.

Following the seeding process, the pearl shell must be handled with great care. After a period where it is rested back in the ocean, and turned over several weeks to facilitate roundness, the shell is taken to grow-out areas where it is hung in panels on long-lines hundreds of metres in length. Over the next two years, and as the pearl shell oyster is a filter feeder, each shell will be carefully cleaned and checked on a monthly basis to ensure that it has open access to food: a highly labour intensive process. Periodically, over this time, x-rays are also conducted to evaluate whether the nucleus has remained in a position that is likely to produce a round pearl.

Harvest time is a time of great activity and great expectation. Farm crew retrieve shell from the long-lines and bring it to the Mother Ship where it is again cleaned and readied for removal of what is hoped to be a stunning round pearl. Where good pearls are recovered, another bead will be inserted "in the hope that the pearl sac with the beautiful nacre secreting cells will produce another beautiful lustrous round pearl in another two years time".[26]

Kailis Australian Pearls' coxswain, Greg Hepple, at harvest time. At harvest time, farm crew work long hours retrieving the pearl shell oyster from long-lines which are then transported to the harvest vessel for subsequent cleaning and recovery of the pearls.

The Kimberley Coast - Pearling

Pearling and the Kimberley Coast

The pearl shell oyster is a filter feeder. Farm crew play a vital role in ensuring that they are regularly cleaned of barnacles and other marine life to ensure their continued ability to feed. In the warm Kimberley waters, marine growth is rapid. Crew start work just after 0500 and work to 1600 on fourteen days on, seven days off, fly-in-fly-out rotations.

The Kimberley Coast - **Pearling**

3. Kimberley Tides

A discussion of the Kimberley's coastal areas would be deficient if there were not to be a consideration of its huge tides. Freshwater Cove, near Doubtful Bay some 250 kilometres to the north of Derby, is home to the largest tides in the southern hemisphere and the second largest in the world. There, the variation between the highest and lowest tides is a staggering vertical depth of 13.8 metres. Only Canada's Bay of Fundy (15 metres) has larger tides, though Great Britain's Severn Estuary (13 metres) comes close.[27] Derby receives the fourth largest tides in the world. In contrast, and only a couple of thousand kilometres to the south, the smallest tides of the Indian Ocean rim are found near Fremantle. There, the tidal variation is just 0.6 metres.[28]

Tides influence everyday life on the Kimberley coast. They determine the routes taken to ensure safe navigation. They determine the location of boat anchorages and they determine the visibility and menace posed by the thousands of submerged reef systems: many of which to this day remain unsurveyed. It is not uncommon for a reef to be fully exposed and then covered in 8 metres of water within a single 6-hour tidal cycle. Even in blue water, navigating the Kimberley coast is treacherous.

What causes the Kimberley's huge tides is a function of a number of factors, some of which are beyond the scope of this text. They reflect the extent and shape of the offshore continental shelf, that extends for some 200 – 300 kilometres into the Timor Sea, and the shape and depth of the Kimberley's thousands of bays and inlets. As tidal forces from the several thousand metre depths of the Timor Sea hit the shallower several hundred metre depths of the continental shelf, a large volume of water is constricted and squeezed. The height and flow of the water must therefore increase to enable it to "fit" the shallower depths of the Kimberley coast.

The top of the black line see here represents the high water mark in the vicinity of the Yampi Peninsula in the Buccaneer Archipelago. One must exercise extreme vigilance in paying attention to tidal movements and heights when using boats along the Kimberley coast, as a skipper of mine failed to do to our detriment on one such occasion. Fortunately, we were able to mobilise the boat through brute force and the use of logs as rollers. When we returned four hours later, the spot in which we had been stuck was about six metres above the water: a sobering thought!

The Kimberley Coast - **Kimberley Tides**

Kimberley tides

The intricate winding patterns seen here at Willie Creek are the creation of water run-off on a falling spring tide. The word "spring" – referring to the period of largest tidal movement in the lunar cycle – is derived from the original meaning of the word, "a flowing of water". The term "neap" means "scanty or lacking" and neap tides refer to the periods of the lunar cycle in which tidal movement is least.

The Kimberley Coast - **Kimberley Tides**

4. King George Falls

The area around the King George River received world attention in 1932. Two German aviators, Hans Bertram and Adolph Klausmann, on a trip from Timor to Darwin, were forced during a storm to put down their Junkers seaplane off the coast at Seaplane Bay, halfway between the King George and Berkeley Rivers. The next 39 days told a story of incredible endurance by two men totally unprepared for Australia's most brutal terrain.

Expecting to find civilisation within hours, and believing they were in the Northern Territory, the two aviators set out on foot heading east without food or water.

We started off on these three days, well shaved, with good shoes and all our baggage, hoping to reach a town within a few hours. At the end, we were walking naked and bare-footed, hungry and with our tongues swollen, and in danger of becoming crazy through lack of water.[29]

After 3 days of walking, the two aviators had found neither water nor civilisation and determined to return to their aircraft. There, they knew that they would be able to get water from its coolant. By this time, a massive land, sea and water search had been initiated by authorities concerned with their non-arrival. The return trip took four days during which they were challenged by the discomfort of thousands of mosquito and sand-fly bites and the need to cross the many crocodile-populated creeks that so characterise the north Kimberley coast.

Upon their arrival back at the aircraft, Bertram and Klausmann fashioned a sailing boat from one of the seaplane floats and headed west: further away from civilisation. Five agonising days were spent at sea during which they did not sight land: their rudder had broken and they had been blown out to sea. During this time they came within close contact of a steamer and search aircraft without being sighted. At the end of the fifth day Bertram used his compass to locate landfall and headed for the coast thinking that they were near Melville Island, to the north of Darwin. On reaching land they set out on foot in what they thought was the direction of Port Cockburn. Once again, they were heading further away from civilisation.

At King George Falls, the King George River plunges 80 metres from the Kimberley Plateau into tidal waters of the King George Gorge. It was discovered by a private explorer, C. Price Conigrave on 7 December 1911. It takes its name from King George V of England whose coronation took place in the same year (though he had acceded to the throne on the death of King Edward VII the previous year).[31] *The Kimberley's European history is so very recent, though its Aboriginal heritage is not.*

The Kimberley Coast - **King George Falls**

By the time Bertram realised where they were (heading inland from the north Kimberley coast) the turquoise waters of the Timor Sea were 3 days behind them and they had been lost for 26 days. Again they headed back to the Junker. This time they would re-rig their float and sail down the Cambridge Gulf to Wyndham where they would find the civilisation that they had thought so near on first leaving the aircraft. Further disaster awaited them. During their absence from the aircraft, high tides and strong winds had battered the plane against rocks making the rejuvenation of their sailing boat difficult at best, unattainable at worst.

Sixteen days after their disappearance, two Aborigines paddled out and met Father Cubero from the then Drysdale River Mission (now Kalumburu) as he anchored off the north Kimberley coast. They showed a handkerchief and cigarette case inscribed with the initials "HB". The remoteness of the location, and the lack of today's more sophisticated communication devices, meant that it was another 13 days before a massive ground, water and air search could be implemented within the area that the personal effects had been found.

On day 39, nearly six weeks after setting out from Timor, Bertram and Klausmann were found by an Aboriginal search party from the Forrest River Mission (now Oombulgurri). Having managed to get the float and sail working, the two had been forced to abandon their attempt to sail to Wyndham and set down in a cave where they hoped that death would arrive quickly. Bertram returned a hero. Klausmann never recovered and spent his last days in an asylum in Germany.[30]

5. King Cascade

King Cascade is one of the Kimberley's most beautiful waterfalls and sits at the head of a natural amphitheatre fringed by mangroves and ferns to the south side of the Prince Regent River. The falls achieved international prominence in 1987 when a 25 year-old American and former model, Ginger Meadows, was taken by a 3 metre saltwater crocodile while swimming at their base.

In the course of evacuating the body by boat, and while anchored for the evening in a tributary of the Prince Regent, a crocodile leapt 1.5 metres out of the water and tried to drag the body-bag off the front of the boat into the river. A shot was fired to fend it off but an hour and a half later, a crocodile leapt again and tore the end out of the bag. The crew upped anchor and moved into the rougher, but comparatively safer, open waters of the St George Basin.

Much has been said about why anyone would take the risk of swimming in such an apparently perfect crocodile habitat. The waters at the base of the falls are tidal and complemented by mangroves on either side. Only those that were present that day can answer that question. However, it is important to remember that the crocodile risk was not as widely publicised then and the crocodile population was still recovering from the days of hunting that had challenged its survival. Even today, it is not uncommon to go for long periods in crocodile populated waters without seeing a single animal. This can, and does, build a sense of complacency that one must constantly watch for; especially when burdened with the pressures imposed by oppressive heat and cool blue waters.

King Cascade

King Cascade was discovered by Captain Philip Parker King during his 1820 voyage in the "Mermaid" though it is unclear as to who named it. The Prince Regent River is the eroded remains of the longest single straight fault-line in Australia. Pioneer pastoralists, Joseph Bradshaw and Aeneas Gunn established a homestead at Marigui, near the mouth of the Prince Regent River, in 1891. Their account is recorded in <u>Under a Regent Moon</u> by Tim Willing and Kevin Kenneally and is a fantastic read: particularly, Gunn's command and colourful use of the English language.

The Kimberley Coast - **King Cascade**

6. Horizontal Waterfall

The Horizontal Waterfall has the potential to become a natural attraction of international significance, particularly if recent front-page national press coverage continues.

Located in Talbot Bay in the Buccaneer Archipelago, the Horizontal Waterfall occurs through two narrow openings: one in each of parallel sandstone ridgelines. On a rising or falling tide, water banks up on one side of the ridgelines. The flow of water through the gaps cannot keep pace with the rate of the rise or fall of the tide and creates a waterfall as it rushes through and down to the lower water levels of the other side. After a short period at the turn of the tide, the process is repeated, though this time in reverse.

It is thought that the two openings through which the waterfalls occur were probably created where the waters of the Archipelago first penetrated the sandstone ridgelines along cracks or joints. These were then eroded such that gaps with widths of 9 and 23 metres were created. Like much of the Buccaneer Archipelago, the effects of intense buckling and folding between 1000 – 560 million years ago are clearly evident. The sandstone cliffs exhibit rock that has been tilted to nearly vertical.

My first view of the power of the Horizontal Waterfall was from the bow of a 4.5 metre dinghy during the Dry season of 2000. While positioning the boat to enable me to take a number of photographs, my skipper, Theo, inadvertently backed into one of the many whirlpools that characterise the area around the waterfall and nearly sank the boat!

The Kimberley Coast - **Horizontal Waterfall**

7. Buccaneer Archipelago

Like the Bonaparte Archipelago to its north-east, and the Kimberley coast more generally, the 800 – 1,000 island Buccaneer Archipelago is a national treasure; and not only for its stunning natural beauty. Populations of flora and fauna, rare or extinct on the mainland, have remained on these islands virtually unaffected by the impacts of fire and the introduction of exotic species brought about since the arrival of European man.

The islands of the Archipelago are characterised by very occasional white sandy beaches and rugged very old King Leopold Sandstone that exhibits severe buckling and folding and some separation along fault-lines. The islands of the Archipelago were created by rising sea levels following the end of the last Ice Age around 18,000 years ago. The rate of rise of sea levels was so rapid that it is estimated that the shores of the Kimberley coast retreated inland at the rate of fifteen metres annually with sea levels rising at the rate of around fifteen millimetres annually. As sea levels rose, so too did the climate become warmer and wetter and, as a result, the flora expanded to incorporate large tracts of monsoon forest; remnants of which remain today.

Mud-stone is a fine-grained sedimentary rock made up of clay particles. The clay can come from weathered granite or from volcanic rocks, including volcanic ash. Weathered granite tends to be the most common.

The Kimberley Coast - **Buccaneer Archipelago**

Buccaneer Archipelago

At least 19 species of native mammals and 25 species of reptiles – including a sub-species of the Taipan - are known from the Archipelago. Over 118 species of birds have been recorded on Koolan Island (one of the largest islands in the Archipelago) alone.[32] The Archipelago was named on 20 August 1821 by Captain Philip Parker King to commemorate William Dampier's visit to the Kimberley coast in 1688.[33]

The Kimberley Coast - **Buccaneer Archipelago**

Buccaneer Archipelago

The northern entrance to Whirlpool Passage. Whirlpool Passage divides Chambers and Hidden Islands in the Buccaneer Archipelago and is characterised at times of peak tidal movement by large boils, metre deep whirlpools and flows running in excess of 15 knots. Passing through the Passage in a small boat when the tide is running is a dramatic but spectacular experience. It was named in March 1838 by Captain John Wickham during his voyage in the Beagle. He noted:

We experienced violent whirlpools, the first of which, from want of experience handled us very roughly, suddenly wrenching the oars out of the men's hands, and whirling the boat around with alarming rapidity.[34]

The Kimberley Coast - **Buccaneer Archipelago**

Buccaneer Archipelago

Sandstone detail in the Buccaneer Archipelago.

The Kimberley Coast - **Buccaneer Archipelago**

Lemon Sharks were constant companions during a stay in the Buccaneer Archipelago, moving with the boat hoping to receive food scraps at the end of each fishing day.

G Derby and the Gibb River Road

1. Introduction

The Gibb River Road extends for 670 kilometres from Derby to the Great Northern Highway, 50 kilometres south of Wyndham. Its creation was due largely to a Commonwealth Government initiative during the early 1960s that was directed at promoting beef production: the Beef Roads Scheme. Millions of dollars were allocated to fund the improvement of both the Duncan Highway and the Great Northern Highway between Wyndham and Halls Creek. Funds were also committed to enable the construction of a new road linking Derby, Mt House, Glenroy and Gibb River Stations: a road that was to become known as the Gibb River Road.

Gibb River itself, and from which the road takes its name, was named by Charles Crossland (second in command of Frederick Brockman's North-west Kimberley Exploring Expedition) on 18 September 1901 after his accomplice, government geologist, A. Gibb Maitland.[35] Crossland and Maitland "made a survey toward Mt Horace and Mt Bernie when they came across:

'…a large stony river running Northwards towards the Drysdale, which carries a great volume of water during flood time. Mr Maitland subsequently traversed this from its junction with the Drysdale. This I have named the Gibb River.'"[36]

A typical late afternoon storm during the "Build-up" on the Gibb River – Kalumburu Road. Strong wind gusts accompany the wonderfully invigorating smell of coming rain that can only be properly appreciated if one has lived through the long rainless months of the Dry

Derby and the Gibb River Road - **Introduction**

Introduction

Prior to the launch of the Beef Roads Scheme, the Gibb River Road was a track that extended between Derby and Napier Downs Stations: a distance of around 130 kilometres. In order to get their cattle to market, the stations of Mt House, Glenroy and Gibb River were required to drove their cattle long distances through sometimes rugged and extreme terrain. In 1949, in an effort to overcome these challenges, abattoirs were opened at Glenroy, about 100 kilometres to the east of the current Aboriginal community of Imintji. In what became known as the "Air Beef Scheme" slaughtered animals were chilled and flown to Wyndham for export to the United Kingdom.

The first section of the Gibb River Road, linking Derby and Glenroy Station, was started in 1961, and in 1963 the first load of frozen beef carcasses travelled to Derby. Within a short time, the road had been extended to Gibb River and the Air Beef Scheme had ended. A key construction challenge was the limited availability of soil. The northern section of the Gibb River road, linking Gibb River and Wyndham, and linking Kalumburu and the Gibb Road, was completed in 1977. Since that time, there has been a progressive upgrading of various parts of the road and the access roads linking stations along its length.

Early morning reflections on the Carson River. On the morning that this photograph was taken, I had just finished a drive of 400 kilometres to deliver three piglets that had been caught by a chopper pilot while mustering on Mt House Station. Their squealing kept me awake the entire night!

Derby and the Gibb River Road - **Introduction**

2. Cattle

At the end of 2001, the Kimberley was home to some 531,000 cattle across a total of 98 pastoral stations covering 23 million hectares and varying in size from 3,000 to 500,000 hectares. Thirty-one of these, incorporating an area of 6.7 million hectares, were held by Aboriginal interests. As at 2001, the Kimberley held the largest number of cattle of any region in Western Australia and around 25% of the State's total herd. An average of 12 – 18% of these cattle are "turned-off" annually with the majority of these cattle being destined for export to Indonesia, Malaysia and the Middle East.[37]

The Kimberley cattle industry owes its foundation to Nathaniel Buchanan who, in 1884, arrived with 4,000 head of Shorthorn cattle after having walked them from Queensland on behalf of the owners, Osmond and Panton. Over the last twenty years or so, much of the Shorthorn (a European breed) herd has been replaced with more profitable and climate suitable Bos Indicus-type cattle (eg, Brahman).

Bos Indicus-type cattle have a number of characteristics that make them more able to withstand the hot humid climate of the tropics than their European counterparts. These include:
(a) a short thick glossy goat that reflects many of the sun's rays and enables it to graze during the heat of the day;
(b) more highly developed sweat glands and an ability to perspire more freely;
(c) the production of an oily secretion in their skin that may help repel insects;
(d) loose skin that increases the body surface area exposed to cooling;
(e) the fact that they produce less internal body heat; and,
(f) a large hump over the top of the shoulder and neck that is comprised of fat, gristle and beef and that serves as a reservoir (in the same way as the hump(s) of a camel) in times of limited feed and/or water.[38]

One of northern Australia's premier bull-catchers, Kurt Hammer, drafts wild scrub bulls for "tipping" and loading, prior to export, on famous Mt House Station. Many bulls weigh more than 550 kilograms and can be extremely dangerous for those failing to take proper care.

Derby and the Gibb River Road - Cattle

Cattle

Leading Kimberley contract musterer, Robert Gray, and Fitzroy Helicopter's Anthea Henwood chase down two wild scrub bulls. This work can be extremely dangerous. Helicopters must locate and flush out often-wild cattle that cannot be mustered by more traditional means. When a bull is flushed out onto the flat, a cut-down short-wheel base Toyota with an oversize bull-bar (often with tyres attached) must then chase the bull down at speed. Upon pulling alongside, the driver must turn into the shoulder of the bull until the bull is knocked over and pinned beneath the bull-bar. What makes the job so difficult is that the driver must drive through scrub characterised by hidden termite mounds, fallen trees, gullies and spear-grass sometimes in excess of two metres. The whole exercise is a real adrenaline kick. On the day that this photograph was taken, I sat in the bull-catcher while we chased down a couple of bulls. The first bull we rolled determined not to run and, at speed, charged the vehicle in which we were travelling at speed, colliding heavily head-on with the bull-bar..

Derby and the Gibb River Road - Cattle

Cattle

"Cowboy" sits atop the drafting yard while wild Short-Horn bulls are processed by Kurt Hammer on Mt House Station. A month or two after, when I bumped into "Cowboy" in Kununurra, "Cowboy" was nursing steel braces in both arms. A set of portable panels, weighing about forty kilograms each, had collapsed on him while loading the equipment truck.

Derby and the Gibb River Road - **Cattle**

Even after the bull has been rolled, risks remain. The legs of the bull must be strapped quickly before it gets up, until a truck can be mobilised to come and collect it. The horns must be "tipped". And even then, some bulls still get up and can hop along at great speed!

3. El Questro Wilderness Park

El Questro Wilderness Park is a testament to the vision and work of its owners and founders, Will and Celia Burrell. Since their purchase of the station in 1991 they have turned the property into a tourist attraction of international repute. Its exclusive homestead offers guests stunning views of Chamberlain Gorge. Natural thermal springs, lush gorges and waterfalls, and the beauty of the Cockburn Range (see later pages), complement what must surely be among the highest concentration of natural beauty to be found anywhere in Australia.

El Questro owes its foundation and naming to Torrance McMicking, who in 1958 was granted a pastoral lease over the area. It is thought that the name El Questro may be a corruption of the Spanish word 'cuesta' meaning a ridge or hill with a steep slope on one side and a gentle slope on the other. More than 700 species of plants and 60 species of mammals have been recorded within the Park's boundaries.[39] The Karunjie Track flanks the western perimeter of the Cockburn Range and was once used as a stock route when droving cattle to the Wyndham meatworks.

Zebedee Springs are unique. Maintaining a consistent temperature of around 32^0C it is thought that they are the product of rainwater that fell hundreds of years ago.[37] This water drained into subterranean hot areas and has then forced its way to the surface under pressure.

Emma Gorge, like much of the El Questro Wilderness Park, is a stunning tropical oasis sheltered amongst the towering sandstone cliffs of the Cockburn Range. On the left-hand side of the gorge can be found numerous examples of rock-art from the Wandjina period, and, at its end lies a pristine droplet waterfall that plunges 30 metres into a crystal-clear rock-pool. Celia Shelmerdine has produced a wonderful coffee-table book, El Questro: A Million Acres of Outback in the Kimberley Wilderness, for those seeking to learn more about El Questro's many hidden secrets.

Derby and the Gibb River Road - **El Questro Wilderness Park**

El Questro Gorge is perhaps my favourite El Questro Gorge. Characterised by lush greenery for much of its length, the magnificent turquoise pool at its head is one of the Kimberley's most difficult photographic challenges. The pool seen here photographs best with a light covering of cloud (cloud diffuses light and helps mitigate the problems of contrast in deep narrow chasms such as El Questro Gorge), meaning that the Wet season offers the greatest photographic opportunities. On the day that this photograph was taken, it took me four attempts to cross a flooded creek and my walk out of the gorge was made difficult by light rain and slippery rocks.

4. Kalumburu

The story of Kalumburu is one of paradoxes. Initially, the Kalumburu missionaries were viewed by local Aboriginal peoples with some suspicion. This was perhaps driven by earlier clashes that had taken place with pearlers operating along the north Kimberley coast in which numerous Aboriginal people had been killed. In 1913, one of the missionaries was speared.

By 1926 the aversion with which the missionaries had earlier been viewed was beginning to fracture. The mission represented an inadvertent challenge to established, and timeless, Aboriginal hierarchies and laws and those with most to gain (women, young people and the outcast) viewed it with a sense of opportunity. Tobacco had become "'the greatest prize in any celebration' as 'Aborigines had acquired a taste for it, and regarded it as a food'".[41] The rationing of this, together with the promise of food, clothing and shelter afforded the missionaries a degree of control that eventually lead to a community characterised by thriving market gardens and virtual total self sufficiency.

In recent years, the degree of discipline that once so characterised Kalumburu has broken down. And for a community that survived Japanese bombing raids in 1943 - 6 people were killed when the Japanese mistook the Kalumburu mission for air-force headquarters which had been concealed at the other end of the airstrip - the future may offer considerable challenges. As for the rest of the Kimberley, the real issue for policy-makers will be to reconcile western, goal-oriented values with those of a culture for which the attainment of economic wealth is of very limited importance. For many Aboriginal people, the living of the day is often far more important than the western concept of "getting ahead".

Kalumburu is sometimes cut-off from road access for up to seven months of the year. It was originally established at Pago, 30 kilometres to the north of its present site, by Spanish Benedictine monks in 1908 before being moved to its present site in 1927. The settlement's name was changed to Kalumburu in 1991 to reflect the fact that the settlement incorporated the entire Kalumburu community and not just the mission.

Derby and the Gibb River Road - **Kalumburu**

5. Mitchell Falls

Mitchell Falls, like nearby Surveyors Pool, form part of the recently gazetted Mitchell River National Park. The Park takes in an area of 115,325 hectares and virtually all of the pre-European flora and fauna remains intact.[42] To date, at least 39 different species of mammals have been recorded (the highest in the State for an area of this size) and the fan palm, *Livistona eastonii*, occurs only on the Mitchell Plateau.[43] During a 1972 field-trip more than 219 species of birds were recorded[44]: nearly 1/3 of Australia's total number of bird species.

Prior to 1942, when the threat of war necessitated evacuation to missions at Kalumburu and Kunmunya, to the Plateau's south, the area was home to the Wunambal people. They exploited the rich and varied food-sources of the offshore islands through the use of rafts made from mangrove wood and food sources included turtle, dugong, molluscs, wild-honey, turtle, kangaroos and wild-turkey. The area averages 1600mm of rainfall annually (the highest in the State) and is home to an astonishing number of Aboriginal art, burial and ceremonial sites.

During the 1960s, a township was proposed for Lone Dingo at the northern end of the Plateau, if and when it could be established that mining of the area's vast bauxite reserves was economically feasible. Fortunately, this never came to fruition. Today, following gazettal of the area as a national park, one of the key challenges lies in containing vast annual wildfires. These are initiated largely by human hand and each Dry season decimate much of the Kimberley; including its precious remnant rainforest pockets.

Mitchell Falls have been created where the Mitchell River drains part of the Kimberley Plateau into Admiralty Gulf via Walmsley Bay. The River continues to actively erode its bed through King Leopold Sandstone. The Mitchell Plateau's wide diversity of habitats, including its many rainforest pockets, and its generally longer wet season, make the area one of the most important habitats for wildlife in the Kimberley.

The Mitchell River was discovered by Government surveyor William Easton in July 1921 and was named by him; most probably after Sir James Mitchell, then Premier and Minister for Lands.[45]

Derby and the Gibb River Road - **Mitchell Falls**

6. Bradshaw Rock-art

The rock-art Europeans refer to as the "Bradshaws" was discovered by Joseph Bradshaw during his 1891 expedition from Wyndham to the Prince Regent River to inspect his newly acquired pastoral lease. It is distinguished by its artistic flowing brush-like figures and is generally characterised by dark red pigments: though other pigments are sometimes seen.

While Bradshaw period art has been dated to be at least 17,000 years old, via the removal and dating of a fossilised wasp-nest overlying one site, it is likely that the art is many years older. It is almost certain that thousands of sites were lost at the end of the last Ice Age 18,000 years ago. Then, sea levels rose up to 180 metres and the coastline moved inland up to 200 kilometres over a period of 11,000 years.[46] And it would seem highly probable that the originators of the rock-art would have inhabited these outer-lying coastal areas first. What makes the Bradshaw art so difficult to date is that the pigments used have entered the rock itself and their composition cannot be determined.

Much of the rock-art from this period is concentrated in the north Kimberley: particularly, around the Mitchell Plateau. In recent years, the privately-owned Kimberley Foundation has acquired a number of north-Kimberley cattle stations with a view to protecting what is an asset of international importance. The Bradshaw period rock-art acts as an historical documentation of events and lives in millennia gone by.

For those wishing to learn more about this art, the Bradshaw Foundation has produced an informative and very affordable CD-Rom which can be purchased through their website at www.bradshawfoundation.com

Derby and the Gibb River Road - **Bradshaw Rock Art**

7. The Spirit Wandjina

Some Kimberley Aboriginal peoples believe that the Wandjinas originated during the "Dreamtime" and wandered the earth creating the streams and rivers, plains and mountains and gorges and waterfalls that we now see today. When their work was complete they retired to the earth and left imprints in the stone. These are the rock paintings that we see today. It is said that they continued to live at the bottom of the waterholes associated with their paintings and that for every Wandjina site there is an associated waterhole.

The Wandjina is believed to be the producer of new child seeds which are regarded as the source of human life: that "dreaming" rather than the act of sexual intercourse determines reproduction. It is believed that the father of a child has to find it in a dream. This appears to him in the shape of his personal totem (usually an animal or a plant). The child's soul will then be passed to his wife in a second dreaming act.

It is said that each Wandjina has a living representative among a clan-group. This is usually an older man that bears the name of the Wandjina that gave him his life spirit and it is this person that is responsible for the custodianship of that site. Wandjina paintings are regarded as centres of spiritual and biological energy bringing the great rains and floods that so regenerate Kimberley life. In days gone past great importance was placed on "touching them up" or renewing the painting. This was to renew the energies they harboured, although this ritual could only be performed during the wet. The arrival of European man, and the subsequent westernisation of Aboriginal culture, has largely caused this ritual to disappear.[47]

Various explanations have been advanced for the absence of a mouth in Wandjina paintings. One school of thought suggests that the mouth should not be painted for to do so would destroy the painting's potency and invite unrelenting rain. Another suggests that the Wandjina marked the sites of skull burials where people found their 'soul' home: that the Wandjinas were portraits of buried and painted skulls. Skulls seen at many burial sites tend to have their lower jaws missing. The halo was said to represent the great cumulus clouds and lightning of the northern monsoon.

Derby and the Gibb River Road - **The Spirit Wandjina**

8. The Charnley River

I have made three trips into the Charnley River (discovered and named by Frank Hann in 1898 after Wallace Charnley of Nullagine). The first, in 1999, was to be undertaken with friends but ended up becoming a solo hike when my friends determined that the threats posed by crocodiles and snakes was too great. That hike remains among the most difficult that I have ever undertaken. The Edkins Range, which divides the Charnley and Calder Rivers (I had parked my vehicle on the northern side of the Calder), offers some of the most brutal and rugged terrain in the Kimberley. On that occasion, eight kilometres of hiking took me nearly two days, during which I temporarily lost my pack when forced to make a dash to the river to obtain more water.

In July 2000, I helicoptered to the upper reaches of the Charnley and walked it solo with my Labrador, Kanch, for ten days. The scenery, while spectacular was also exhausting, and the trip culminated in the dramatic rescue of Kanch from the face of a sixty metre cliff while my chopper pilot, Bill Boothby, watched on. Pulling Kanch out of a cave, while standing on a ledge not more than forty centimetres wide, with a drop of forty metres straight down, is one of the most challenging situations I have ever dealt with.

In November/ December 2000, I returned again to the Charnley by helicopter with friends Tony Gavranich and Andy Ellett. Temperatures in the gorge, near the junction of the freshwater and the salt, averaged between forty five and fifty degrees daily (attested to by our helicopter's temperature gauge) and we spent most of our time in a shallow rock-pool cooling down: a fantastic experience nevertheless. One evening, we awoke to be surprised by a big spring tide and the sight of a small saltwater crocodile coming out of the water to investigate our sleeping arrangements! Andy and Tony spent the rest of the night atop a boulder to deny the possibility of any further such investigations. What one does in search of a photo!

Some of the Kimberley's most spectacular, yet rugged, scenery is inaccessible other than by

Derby and the Gibb River Road - **The Charnley River**

9. Manning Gorge

Manning Gorge has been carved by Manning Creek (named after Mr Manning of Lennard River in 1895) on Mt Barnett Station 300 kilometres north-east of Derby. In times past, it formed a popular meeting place and fishing hole for local Aboriginal peoples who tended never to live far from permanent water. A serious strain of influenza is said to have afflicted the area, and nearby Gibb River Station, in the late 1920s or early 1930s. As many as 90% of the native Aboriginal peoples, with no in-built immunity to European diseases, are said to have died. They were "lying in waterholes and dying like flies". By the early 1950s, only a handful of Aboriginal people lived a traditional bush lifestyle. Those that had survived the "flu" worked the nearby stations.[48]

Mt Barnett Station is owned by the local Kupungarri Aboriginal Community. The station takes it name from Alfred Barnett who moved to the Kimberley in 1882. After managing Meda Station near Derby, Mr Barnett moved to manage Balmaningarri Station on the relatively close Lennard River where he remained until 1905. He was well-liked by local Aboriginal peoples and saved a number of lives, including two white men and a number of Aborigines, during the floods of 1895. In his time in the Kimberley, Barnett is said to have learned the local Aboriginal language and attended a number of corroborees.[49]

With today's modern conveniences, it is easy to overlook the challenges that faced our pioneer pastoralists. Prior to the construction of the Gibb River Beef Road, stores were flown in by DC3 to nearby Gibb River Station. Stations were allowed a maximum of six drums of diesel on each flight and, if they ran out, "it was back on the horse again".[50] Prior to it becoming a major tourist attraction, the Gorge acted as the host to an annual Boxing Day cricket match for local pastoralists.

Derby and the Gibb River Road - **Manning Gorge**

10. Bell Gorge

Bell Gorge is located in the King Leopold Ranges on Bell Creek (discovered and named by Frank Hann in 1898 after Mr Bell of Derby), about 300 metres above sea level. What became apparent during my research into this area, and the King Leopold Ranges more generally, was the minimal amount that is still known about the flora and fauna of the area. This is evidenced by the ease with which scientists have been able to discover unidentified flora and fauna in their limited visits. Far more research is required. Discussions with the WA Museum have indicated that the area, like much of the north-west Kimberley, is rich in its diversity of mammal species. In two nights trapping during one field trip, they captured six mammal species that included the Northern Native Cat and the Bandicoot. In recent times further detailed studies have also been undertaken into the abundant Northern Long Necked Turtles that live within the Park, though the findings of those studies have not yet been published.

The King Leopold Ranges take their name from King Leopold of Belgium. They were discovered and named by Alexander Forrest during his travels of 1879 and were not successfully traversed by Europeans until Frank Hann found a way through during his explorations of 1898. Like the islands comprising the Buccaneer Archipelago, the steep hills and ridges of the King Leopolds are developed in a thick sequence of layered rocks. The most abundant of these are white and pink quartz sandstone, buff siltstone and brown mudstone, the sediment of which started to accumulate in the Kimberley Basin - a basin is a low area in the earth's crust - 1.8 billion years ago. This sequence of rocks is more than 5 kilometres thick. About 560 million years ago, these sedimentary rocks were thrust over older granite, volcanic and metamorphosed sedimentary rocks of the Hooper Complex to the south-west. This caused the rocks at the leading edge to buckle into a major mountain chain, the eroded remnants of which now exist as the King Leopold Ranges and the islands of the Buccaneer Archipelago.

The King Leopold Ranges Conservation Park, of which Bell Gorge is a part, was gazetted on 10 July 2000. This photograph proved to be one of the most difficult in the book, and even now, I remain unhappy with the result. At the start of the 2004 wet season, an A$1,100 helicopter charter proved unsuccessful when mechanical problems necessitated we return to Fitzroy and get another machine. The resulting delay meant that we had "lost the light" by the time we reached the gorge. Two weeks later, I returned. The falls were quite spectacular.

Derby and the Gibb River Road - **Bell Gorge**

11. Lennard River Gorge

At Lennard Gorge, the Lennard River plunges 30 metres into a spectacular narrow gorge then steep-sided chasm. Extreme care should be exercised when negotiating the Gorge walls, particularly on the southern side, as they are coated with a slippery grey lichen. I was fortunate to walk away from a 13 metre fall in 1999, when I slipped on this lichen and fell over the waterfall onto my back below. My diary records:

At first, I clawed my fingers into the rock to stop me falling, but then realising that it was no use decided that it was best not to resist and so let myself go with the fall. It's quite funny the thoughts that go through your head during incidents like this....As I approached the second half of the fall (I fell a total distance of 13 metres), and knowing that there would be no water to break my fall, but rather rocks at the bottom, my mind moved toward "now what is going to happen here? What am I going to break?... When I gathered myself - I was not sure what I had broken – the waterfall started to push me down into the pool below..... I got worried. Because I had landed on my back very hard, I was not sure if I had broken my back and that perhaps my legs wouldn't work.

And photography is said to be a passive occupation!

The Lennard River originates in the King Leopold Ranges and was discovered by Alexander Forrest on 8 June 1879 during his expedition from De Grey, near current-day Port Hedland, to Port Darwin.[51] He named it after his fiancee, Amy Barret Lennard.[52] The main pool at Lennard Gorge is home to two harmless Merten's Water Monitors.

Derby and the Gibb River Road - **Lennard River Gorge**

The Australian Boab, *Adansonia gregorii*, is one of 8 species of Baobab. Six of the remaining species are found in Madagascar and the seventh throughout tropical Africa. Famed for its unusual variety of forms, *Adansonia gregorii* is found only in the Victoria River region of the Northern Territory and the Kimberley. The Boab is a deciduous tree, shedding its leaves toward the end of the long Dry season and regaining them again as humidity builds during the hot months of October, November and December. Its flowers come in November and December and are of a pale, creamy yellow colour. They open only at night.

An interesting debate that has gained momentum in recent years relates to the location of the largest boab in the Kimberley. Two specimens that have been put forward include one at the junction of the Sprigg and Isdell Rivers – with a chest-height circumference of around 16 metres – and another on the Dunham River on Kingston Rest Station that has a chest-height circumference of 17.7 metres.[57]

Derby and the Gibb River Road - **Boab Trees**

Boab Trees

The Boab tree holds an important place in traditional Aboriginal life. Especially prior to the arrival of European man, its leaves were often placed in fires to deter mosquitoes and they were sometimes used as a bed on which to place cooked meat and fish. Bark and root fibres were used for making cord, by pounding cut lengths with rock "to make them like wool"[53], and then rolling them against one's thigh with a long string or thicker rope. The pith of the Boab – the white substance contained within the nut – could be crushed and mixed with water and wild honey to produce a cordial-like drink that varied in taste depending upon the sweetness of the pith. Aboriginal people would sometimes cut through the bark of the Boab to access the white wood: strips torn off could be sucked to obtain moisture.

Some Aboriginal groups warned against sleeping under Boabs at night as snakes were said to sleep in the branches. The snakes might fall on them as they slept.[54] Similarly, some did not burn Boab wood as it was said that the tree's light and woody nature might make the person's body light: like the wood itself.[55] A particular tree in the north Kimberley was said to make rain if touched and in other cases it was said that someone intending to harm another would carve an effigy of his victim in the tree's bark and sing a malevolent song. As a result, the victim would blow up to resemble a Boab tree.[56]

Boab reflections on El Questro Station.

Derby and the Gibb River Road - **Boab Trees**

Boab Trees

Night-time in the Kimberley as stars leave their trail above a lonely Boab on Fairfield Station.

Derby and the Gibb River Road - **Boab Trees**

13. Derby

If Halls Creek and Fitzroy Crossing owed their foundation to the finding of gold at Halls Creek, then Derby, like Wyndham, had its genesis in the pastoral industry. This followed the explorations, and subsequent favourable reports, of Alexander Forrest in 1879. By 1883, Derby was a small shanty-town and, for all intents and purposes could lay strong claim to the title of the Kimberley's first town: even if Broome had been officially recognised on 21 November 1883, a day earlier than Derby. In 1888, when Charles Flinders rode through to Oobagooma – 5 years after the 1883 proclamation – he is reported to have said that "There was not one sheet of iron in Broome in '88".[58]

In recent years, proposals have been tendered to upgrade the Derby Port to enable it to dispatch live cattle shipments bound for the markets of Indonesia and Malaysia. These have been rejected though on the basis of Derby's huge tidal range – one of the largest in the world – and the fact that modern ships are not designed to spend time on the ocean bottom. At low tide, the mud bottom of King Sound at the base of Derby jetty is completely exposed.

As Broome has thrived in recent years, so too has Derby been challenged. Perth-based Governments, generally with little understanding of the unique challenges facing the north, have pushed further for more effective allocation of scarce Government resources. This has lead to the centralisation of many services in Broome and their concurrent movement away from Derby. It is an interesting paradigm. On the one hand, and driven by economic and military objectives, Governments of both denominations have pursued many avenues in their attempt to increase the 25,000 strong Kimberley population. On the other, the taking away of many essential services has inhibited these efforts.

From its heyday of 1886, when thousands berthed at Derby en route to the Halls Creek goldfields, Derby is still largely reliant on the pastoral industry. Until very recently, the Port was used as an export facility for bulk ore concentrate mined from the Pillara base metals mine, some 360 kilometres to the town's east. However, in October 2003, the mine was put into shutdown mode to await re-opening upon the improvement of base metal prices and economic conditions.

Derby was named after Edward Henry Stanley, Lord Derby (1826 – 1893), Secretary of State for Colonies between 1882 and 1885. On December 5, 1921, Derby received what is said to have been Australia's first scheduled aviation flight service from Geraldton; a year before Qantas began its flight service from Charleville to Cloncurry.[59]

Derby and the Gibb River Road - **Derby**

14. King Sound

More than 100 kilometres long and around 50 kilometres across at its widest point, King Sound is fed by the Kimberley's longest river, the Fitzroy. At 622 kilometres in length, the Fitzroy has an average annual flow of 8.2 cubic kilometres.[60] King Sound was discovered by Captain Philip Parker King during his 1818 survey of the north Australian coast. He named it Cygnet Bay, but that name was later changed to its current name by Lieutenant John Lort-Stokes during his 1838 voyage in the *Beagle*: the same voyage in which the Fitzroy was discovered and named. Stokes was optimistic that King Sound was the entrance to a vast inland sea that was then thought to exist and that drove much of the early European exploration of the Australian continent.

King Sound is notorious for its savage ripping 10 metre tides and treacherous navigation. However, it is this very feature that provided the stimulant to one of the more interesting proposals put forward in recent years: the Derby Tidal Power Scheme. Under this scheme – which was rejected because of cost - a dam was to be built across the mouth of the east and west arms of Doctors Creek near Derby. Sluice gates were to be incorporated to allow water into the high basin - the west arm - on the rising tide and out of the low basin - the east arm - on the falling tide. A channel containing turbines would be dug between the two arms that would generate electricity for carriage to Derby, Broome, Fitzroy Crossing and the Pillara base-metals mine.

An ancient river delta creates a work of unique natural artistry near Derby at the bottom of King Sound. These spectacular alluvial fans are inundated only on large spring tides with the salt being the evaporative remnants of the water that remained behind after the tide has gone out.

Derby and the Gibb River Road - **King Sound**

H Fitzroy Crossing and the Devonian Reef National Parks

1. Introduction

The popular tourist areas of Windjana Gorge, Tunnel Creek, Geikie Gorge and Mimbi Caves are all contained within an extensive Devonian limestone reef complex that is thought to be around 370 million years old. It extends for 350 kilometres from Napier Downs Station on the Gibb River Road, to Ngumpan Cliffs, 100 kilometres to the east of Fitzroy Crossing.

Incorporated within the reef system are the Napier, Oscar, Geikie, Pillara, Emanuel and Lawford Ranges. It is of immense scientific and cultural importance, being the best example of its kind anywhere in the world. American geologist, Professor C.L. Camp, when writing of the area many years ago, noted that:

> *It runs like an old ruin, black castellated walls for a distance of some forty miles.*[61] *Along the entire length of this escarpment the cliff faces are perforated by cave entrances and fissures. These when partially eaten away by erosion produce the most remarkable and varied rock forms; windows, arches, spires, domes, and pinnacles of continuous interest to the traveller.*[62]

Formation of the Reef system can be traced to the Devonian geological period when all but the eastern parts of the Kimberley were covered by a warm, tropical sea. In these waters, calcareous algae and now-extinct lime-secreting organisms thrived, building an ancient barrier reef to sea level. It was up to one thousand kilometres long and fringed the then coast. As the sea floor subsided, so these reef-building organisms kept building up to maintain their height at sea level. They eventually constructed a reef that was up to two kilometres thick.

Between 310 – 270 million years ago, the Kimberley, and much of Australia, was again affected by an ice age. Sedimentary rocks that formed during this period buried the Devonian Reef. Then, 20 million years ago, the reef was again uplifted. Progressive subsequent weathering and erosion of the softer overlying sedimentary rocks has left the more resistant limestone reef to stand above the surrounding landscape.

Sunset in the Napier Range. We spent much of that afternoon and the following day searching for Cycad Hill (seen in the distance), a conical hill significant for the volume of cycads that live on its slopes. Our topographical maps were inaccurate by a couple of kilometres and we were able to verify this by the absence of cycads other than on the slopes of this single hill.

Fitzroy Crossing and the Devonian Reef National Parks - **Introduction**

2. Windjana Gorge

Located in the Napier Range to the north-east of Derby, Windjana Gorge is 3.5 kilometres long and has been carved to its current 80 metre depth by the seasonal Lennard River. It was originally named Devil's Pass by government geologist, Edward Hardman, during the John Forrest-led expedition of 1883 - as a result of "the difficulties to passage it presents"[63] - before being changed to its current name in the years soon-after. The name 'Windjana' appears to be a corruption of the word 'Wandjina' which is used to refer to the Aboriginal spirit-being that is said to have roamed the earth during the Dreamtime.

Windjana Gorge is regarded by geologists as one of the classic features of world geology due to the relationship between various deposits in the reef complex. It supports a wide variety of flora including Coolamon trees, Leichhardt Pine, figs and Melaleucas (paperbark). The Gorge is home to Corellas, Fruit Bats and the rare Peregrine Falcon. The caves of the Gorge support the rare Yellow-lipped Bat; a flying mammal found only in the Kimberley.

Windjana Gorge is home to a large population of freshwater crocodiles and these can be seen sunning themselves during the cooler months of the Dry season. I am not aware of saltwater crocodiles having been sighted in Windjana Gorge, though it is not inconceivable that they might be found there. It is not a great distance from the waters of King Sound and there appear to be no natural barriers, such as waterfalls, to them pushing up this far during the floodwaters of the Wet. I am aware of saltwater crocodiles having pushed a long-way inland in far more rugged country than that cut by the Lennard River.

During the last 20 years, scientists have been studying the height and age of flood debris left by rivers passing through the Devonian reef. Ancient flood debris are found high in caves in the gorge cliff-lines and age is determined via carbon-dating of the debris particles. By understanding these factors, scientists will be better able to predict the severity, size and frequency of the so-called super-floods. With greenhouse effect modelling predicting that cyclones will travel further south, and the climate in Australia likely to become more erratic, this has implications for the construction of roads, bridges and dams throughout Australia.[64]

Fitzroy Crossing and the Devonian Reef National Parks - **Windjana Gorge**

3. Tunnel Creek

Located in the Oscar Range to the east of Windjana Gorge, Tunnel Creek has carved a one kilometre long cave through the Range. It first gained attention as the favourite hide-out of the Aboriginal outlaw, Jandamarra, or Pigeon as he has become popularly known, during his escapades of the late 19th century.

It is often asserted that Jandamarra was a member of the Bunuba people, although a few ancient sages still claim that he was predominantly of Ungami origin. After being imprisoned for sheep and cattle theft in the late 1880s, he was trained as a tracker by local law enforcement authorities and fulfilled that role with success on and off for a number of years. In 1894, following the arrest of 16 of his countrymen, Jandamarra rebelled without warning. Despite having previously saved the life of his commanding constable, PC Richardson, Jandamarra shot Richardson in his sleep at the Lillimooloora Homestead and set free his countrymen. Soon after, he ambushed a supply wagon and, after killing 2 of the 3 men in charge, escaped with a supply of firearms and other materials.

With the assistance of his clan's people, Jandamarra engaged in a wide-ranging guerrilla war with pastoralists and law enforcement authorities between 1894 and 1897. Battles were fought at Windjana Gorge (a major one in 1894 became known as the battle of Windjana Gorge), Tunnel Creek and Fitzroy Crossing and extended to parts of the King Leopold Ranges. The conflict resulted in the deaths of 6 white people and scores of Aboriginal people. Jandamarra was killed in a shoot-out with his pursuers in the Oscar Range, near Tunnel Creek, in 1897. He was 24.

Tunnel Creek (previously known as Mt North Creek) is home to freshwater crocodiles, fish, cherrabun and a large population of ghost bats. Like the Lennard and Fitzroy Rivers that have carved Windjana and Geikie Gorges, Tunnel Creek runs contrary to the paths of usual limestone waterways that flow parallel with the limestone. These are old streams formed when the limestone reef was capped with sandstone. As the sandstone has eroded the streams have continued to cut their path; this time through the newly exposed limestone reef.

Fitzroy Crossing and the Devonian Reef National Parks - **Tunnel Creek**

4. 'Build-up' time in the Kimberley – Blina Station, Great Northern Highway

The scattered rain shower seen here is typical of the "Build-up" in northern Australia. During this time, high October to December temperatures – in the central Kimberley the average daily maximum is generally in excess of 40 degrees Celsius - heat the north Australian land-mass causing the air above it to heat and rise. As the air rises, the pressure bearing down on it diminishes and the air expands and cools. Water vapour contained within the cooling air starts to condense and cumulus cloud forms. This process of condensation releases large quantities of heat which keeps the air inside the cloud warmer than the surrounding air and causes the cloud to rise further. As the cloud rises, more air is required to replace the air that has risen off the ground. The cloud continues to rise and moist air from around the cloud is sucked in (creating updraughts). The power of these updraughts keeps the water droplets suspended in the air and prevents them from falling until the water droplets become large and heavy and fall as rain.[65]

The familiar anvil shape of the giant thunderhead clouds that so characterise late afternoon "Build-up" skies in northern Australia is the result of the cumulus cloud growing to the limit of the lower atmosphere (the troposphere) and being blown by high level winds.

Fitzroy Crossing and the Devonian Reef National Parks - **Build-up Boab - Blina Station, Great Northern Highway**

5. Geikie Gorge

Geikie Gorge is a creation of the Fitzroy River, carved at the junction of the Devonian-reef formed Oscar and Geikie Ranges. The Fitzroy River was discovered by Lieutenant John Lort-Stokes on 26 February 1838 during his voyage in the *Beagle* to chart the north Australian coast. He named it after Captain Robert Fitz-Roy, the second commander of the *Beagle*. Geikie Gorge was named by Government Geologist, Edward Hardman, in 1883 after Sir Archibald Geikie, Director-General of Geological Survey for Great Britain and Ireland.

Geikie Gorge extends for seven kilometres and is significant not only for its natural beauty, but also for the fact that it forms a major drought refuge for endangered bird species and rare freshwater fishes. The main gorge pool, dug deep by the swirling floodwaters of the Wet, extends to a depth of fifteen metres towards the end of the Dry. It supports freshwater Barramundi, Leichardt's Sawfish and the Coach-whip Stingray. These are species normally found only in salt-water. They are thought to be descendents of marine fishes that were cut off from the sea perhaps a million years ago. The eastern sandbanks of the gorge are a significant breeding habitat for a large population of freshwater crocodiles and cannot be accessed without a permit from CALM.

Geikie Gorge at the end of the "Build-up". Darngku Heritage Cruises is owned and operated by members of the Darngku Aboriginal clan. Their cruises offer an excellent and informative Aboriginal insight to both the meaning of the Gorge to Aboriginal people and its unique flora and fauna.

Fitzroy Crossing and the Devonian Reef National Parks - Geikie Gorge

Geikie Gorge

late afternoon; when the setting sun lights up the east wall. At these times, and particularly during the Dry season months of June, July and August, low pressure systems, with associated cold fronts moving through the Great Australian Bight, bring still windless conditions to the north; particularly in the evenings. The gorge walls glow a warm golden colour that reflect almost perfectly in the still clear waters of the river. Throughout the Gorge, there are numerous underwater springs, and the rock lying in the middle of the southern part of the Gorge, Darngku Rock, is a significant site for the Darngku Aboriginal people, the traditional owners of the area taking in Geikie Gorge.

The grey colour of the Reef is a thin, even, covering of a lichen (*Lichenothelia*) that coats the walls where it has had time to colonise. The clear white line, evident across the entire length of the Gorge, represents the natural colour of the limestone scoured clean by the swirling, silt-carrying floodwaters of the wet. It also represents the maximum height of the wet season flood-waters. The orange stripes represent stains of iron oxide and are areas where the limestone carries insufficient moisture to support lichen growth.

One of many spectacular gorges found throughout the 350 kilometre Devonian limestone reef complex. The reef is also home to extensive above-ground and underground cave systems.

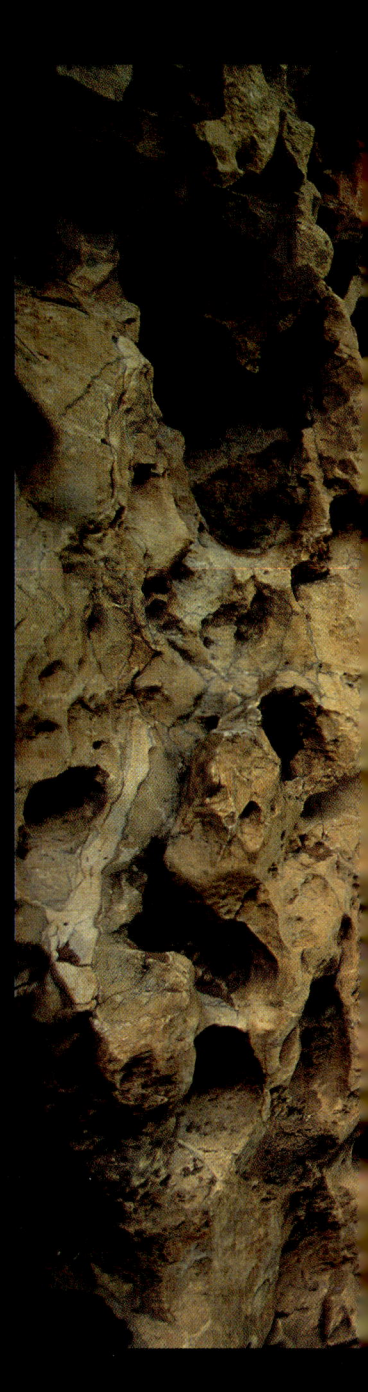

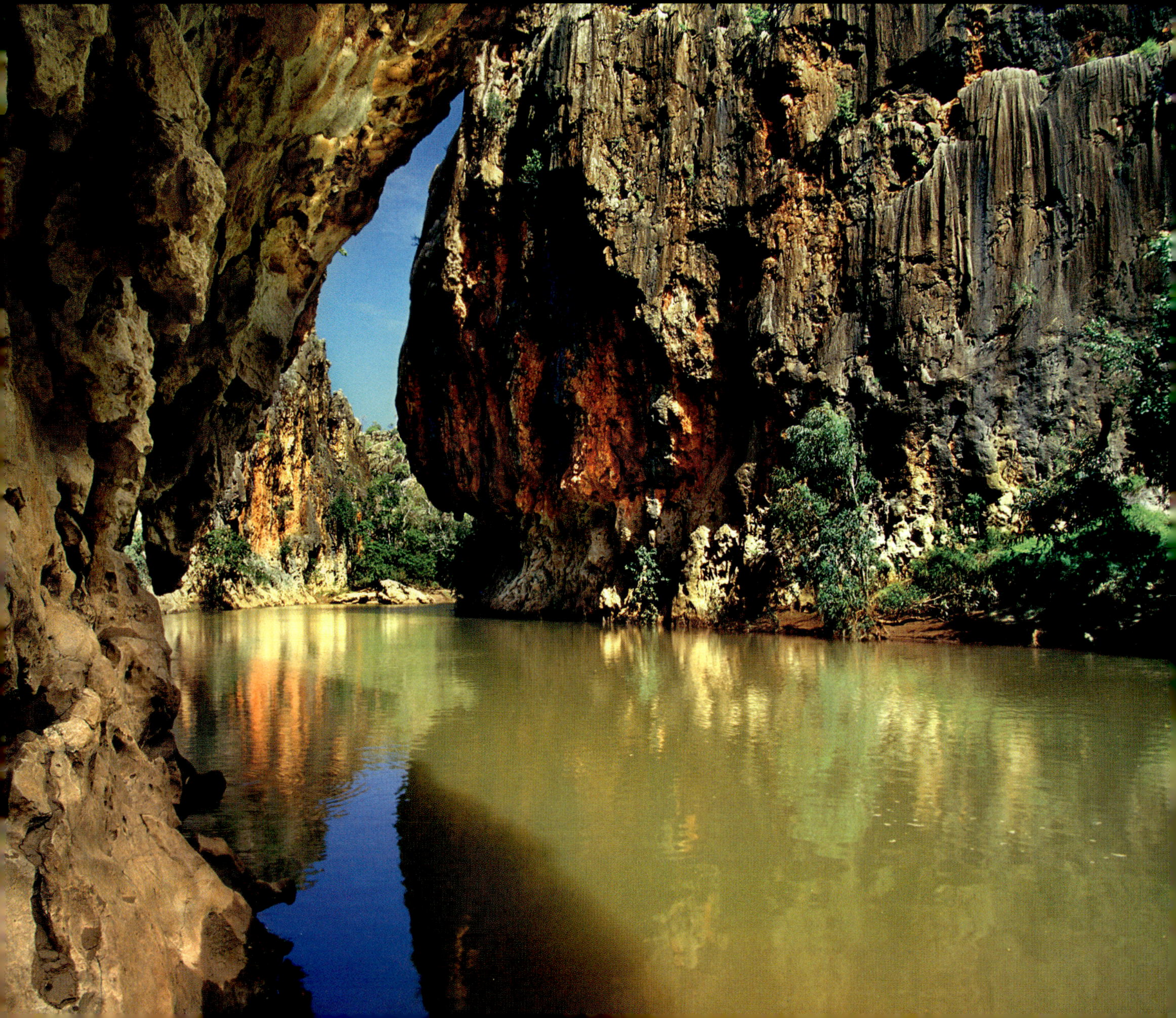

6. Fitzroy Crossing

For a region that is home to only 25,000 people, every Kimberley town has its own very different feel. For me, the enduring memories of Fitzroy Crossing, which has served as my home for the past 18 months, will be of blazing country music being played at five in the morning and sweltering October temperatures. At one stage in 2002 we had four consecutive days of 45 degrees and then two of 44 degrees. They will be watching "Beck" the cow get hounded by local camp dogs as she nibbled on grass outside my office and seeing two emus wander about the main highway oblivious to human presence. They will involve mending radiators with bullet-holes and hearing stories of how good mates got buried at the local cemetery with their heads pointing toward one another and close together "so they could 'talk' to one another". Yes, Fitzroy is one of a kind!

Fitzroy Crossing is home to 1500 mostly Aboriginal people and is essentially an amalgamation of 3 different language groups: Bunuba, Gooniyandi and Walmajarri. Amalgamation posed enormous challenges as it occurred relatively suddenly. In the late 1960s Aboriginal people were forced from stations when the Commonwealth mandated a minimum wage and their continued station employment became cost-prohibitive. The resulting influx of people to towns such as Fitzroy Crossing saw laws that had governed intra and inter-tribal relationships (eg, laws of kinship) break down in the face of challenge from the white-man evils of drugs and alcohol. The traditional enforcers of tribal discipline, the old people, lost control of the young. The fact that the town has achieved what it has is remarkable.

The old Crossing, a low-lying concrete structure, was Fitzroy Crossing's first bridge. As it could be closed for months at a time during the Wet season, it was built up to a wider bridge in 1958. The existing bridge was completed downstream in 1974 and has resulted in a shift away from the old townsite to Fitzroy's current location.

Storms that travel down the Fitzroy catchment create more of a flood risk than those travelling up. For those with an interest in learning more about Kimberley rivers, Kim Epton's (2003) Rivers of the Kimberley is an excellent documentation of the European discovery and naming of each of the Kimberley's 109 rivers.

Fitzroy Crossing and the Devonian Reef National Parks - **Fitzroy Crossing**

Halls Creek and Surrounds

1. Halls Creek

Different in feel to Fitzroy Crossing, although having roughly the same population, Halls Creek owes its existence to the discovery of gold in 1885 by Charlie Hall and John Slattery. The town was originally located 16 kilometres to the east of present-day Halls Creek, close to where the gold was discovered. However, flooding in the Wet season, and a lack of water during the Dry, necessitated its relocation to its existing site.

Although the gold-rush lasted not more than 2 – 3 years, there were, at its peak, at least 3,000 prospectors on the field. One such prospector, John Fredericks, or Russian Jack as he was popularly known, was to achieve immortality for having reportedly pushed a sick man 300 kilometres from Halls Creek to Wyndham in a hand-made, wooden-wheeled, dishevelled wheel-barrow. In fact, and for the sake of the record, Jack pushed the traveller for a distance of between 30 and 60 kilometres from west of Halls Creek to Halls Creek: an incredible feat of human endurance and kindness nevertheless.[66]

Other newspaper reports noted that on a further occasion, and having been arrested for drunkenness in Queensland, Jack was chained to his jail while his captor attended to another job. Jack's jail in this case was a log. Being somewhat thirsty in the heat he decided to up and carry his jail (which was the log) back to the pub. When eventually his captor caught up with him, Jack refused to leave unless he could carry his bottle of brandy with him. "You might keep heem; you putta the brandy in my shirt, then I carry the log and we all go home. If I no getta the brandy then the log stay here in the bar. I getta the bottle."[67]

For those prepared to spend the time, Halls Creek is home to a wealth of history and nearby natural attractions. The Kimberley Hotel contains a selection of historical displays and photos and offers a welcome respite from the harshness of the area's surrounding landscape.

Halls Creek and Surrounds - **Halls Creek**

2. Wolfe Creek Crater

Wolfe Creek Crater has been popularly (but erroneously) said to be the world's second largest meteorite crater. The truth is that while it is the second largest meteorite crater *in or near which actual meteorite fragments have been found,* there are many larger craters both in Australia and around the world. Of the world's 140 known or probable meteorite craters, 23 of these are found in Australia and 5 in the Kimberley.[68]

Meteorite impacts producing craters of the magnitude of Wolfe Creek are predicted to occur once every 25,000 years. Iron meteorite fragments, weighing up to 72.6 grams, have been found about 3.9 kilometres south-west of the crater.[69] The Djaru Aboriginal peoples call the crater "Gandimalal", and tell of two rainbow snakes moving across the land during the Dreamtime. Gandimalal was created when one of the snakes came out of the ground.

Halls Creek and Surrounds - **Wolfe Creek Crater**

Wolfe Creek Crater

Wolfe Creek Crater is almost perfectly round – its diameter varies between 870 and 950 metres – and rises 35 metres above the surrounding desert. It is one of the world's more spectacular meteorite craters and is believed to have been created around 300,000 years ago by a meteorite the size of a 50,000 tonne battleship that was travelling in excess of 500 kilometres per hour. Upon impact, the meteorite vaporised and the resulting transfer of heat melted the rock within the immediate impact area. This gave rise to the rim that is evident today. Now about 50 metres deep, the crater is being filled by the shifting sands of the Tanami Desert. It is believed to have been 150 metres deep at the time of impact.

Wolfe Creek Crater takes its name from nearby Wolfe Creek. Located approximately 100 kilometres to the south of Halls Creek, it was officially recorded by an aerial reconnaissance team in 1947, although locals had known of its existence for many years prior. It has been suggested that the original discoverer of the crater may have been Alec Whitlam – an MMA pilot – who is thought to have discovered the crater somewhere between the 1930s and the early 1950s. By the early 1950s, it was referred to as "Whitlam's Crater" by MMA pilots. However, this name may have been known only to MMA pilots and the name "Wolfe Creek Meteorite Crater" was formally approved on 5 December 1966.

Halls Creek and Surrounds - **Wolfe Creek Crater**

3. Shadow Detail: Osmond Range

A work in progress. Wet season rains etch patterns and gorges in the landscape between Purnululu National Park and the southern tip of Lake Argyle. Alligator Airways fly daily from Kununurra and much of this country is inaccessible from the ground.

4. Lake Gregory

Lake Gregory offers another example of the Kimberley's unique landscape and habitat diversity. Located on the edge of the Tanami Desert, 250 kilometres to the south-south-east of Halls Creek, the Lake contains both spectacular numbers of waterbirds and fresh water when water levels are high. A September 1986 survey recorded 57 bird species and 240,000 individual birds.[70]

Augustus Gregory, after whom the Lake takes its name (though he did not name it) and its discoverer, wrote on 8 March 1856:

> Started at 6.5am and traced the creek into a salt lake to the west… [A]fter having followed Sturt's Creek for nearly 300 miles, we have been disappointed in our hope that it would lead to some important outlet to the waters of the Australian interior; it has, however, enabled us to penetrate far into the level tract of country which may be determined the Great Australian Desert.[71]

5. Albert Edward Range

Related to cockroaches, not ants, termites are herbivores that convert the nutrients from grass and wood into protein. Termite mounds are created by termites cementing grains of soil together with saliva and excreta. They typically contain numerous galleries, along which the termites move, and a royal chamber and nursery at their centre. Australia is home to about 350 of the estimated 2300 termite species globally.[72]

Halls Creek and Surrounds - **Albert Edward Range**

6. Palm Springs

Palm Springs is a natural spring located in the Albert Edward Range about 27 kilometres south-east of Halls Creek. It is a popular swimming spot with locals and is distinctive for its smattering of palms amidst an otherwise harsh landscape. It contains permanent water.

Halls Creek and Surrounds - **Palm Springs**

Saw Tooth Gorge is located only a couple of kilometres from Palm Springs, about 27 kilometres from Halls Creek. It is also a popular swimming spot for locals and contains water for most of the year.

Halls Creek and Surrounds - **Saw Tooth Gorge**

8. China Wall

China Wall takes its name from its more illustrious Chinese namesake for the uncanny likeness it bears to that feature. It extends for many kilometres through the hills around Halls Creek and is a sub-vertical quartz vein that was injected through a fracture in the enclosing sandstone rock. Its higher resistance to weathering has seen it survive the erosion of the surrounding and softer sandstone.

9. Barramundi Fishing

Though a long way inland, Barramundi are found in many of the creeks and rivers around Halls Creek. Growing to a length of over 150cm and weighing up to 50kg, Barramundi spawn in brackish or sea water where the survival of eggs and early stage larvae is dependent upon water with salinity levels of 22 – 40%. After three to six months, juvenile fish will then swim upstream (generally in the later part of the wet season when rivers and creeks are still running) into the freshwater reaches of rivers where they will remain for three to four years and undertake much of their growth. After this time, they will again return to the saltwater reaches where they will then spawn and spend the rest of their lives. In northern Australia, spawning occurs between September and March, with the peak periods being November to December and February to March.

10. Purnululu National Park

I must admit that I avoided going to the 2003 World-Heritage-Listed Bungles for quite some time. Too many people I thought; everyone goes there. Big mistake! When I did eventually make the trip from my home in Fitzroy Crossing, I was immediately struck by its beauty and scale. The Bungles are far, far more than the striped beehive-like domes for which they are internationally famous. For me, the real splendour of the Bungles lies in its deep, *Livistona*-laced chasms and gorges. Plus it was good to enjoy my time from the comfort of my accommodation at the Discover the Kimberley Tours Camp close to the beehives in the south-western part of the Range!

Some Aboriginal groups associated with the Bungles believe that the area's unique beehives and gorges were created as an echidna burrowed to escape the attacks of a galah. The Livistona Palms were the quills that the echidna lost during the attack.

Halls Creek and Surrounds - **Purnululu National Park**

Purnululu National Park

Visitors to the Bungles will notice the marked difference in geology between the coarse conglomerate of the north-western part of the Range and the bee-hive and fine friable sandstone of the south. The conglomerate of the north-western part is characterised by large pebbles, rock and cobbles held together by a sandy cement. These were deposited by high energy streams flowing from the north 360 million years ago. The lighter sands, not so constrained by weight, were deposited around the southern areas of the range. Over a period of approximately 60 million years, these gravels and sands were buried and compacted to a depth of 2 kilometres.

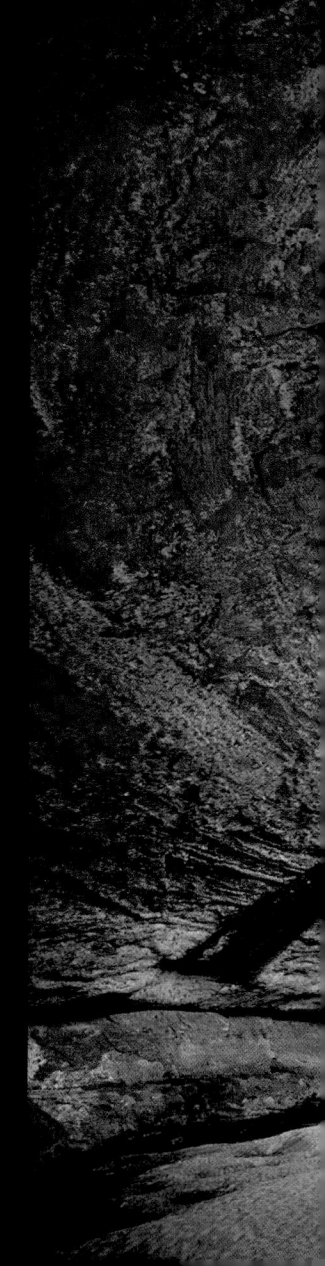

The amphitheatre at the end of Cathedral Gorge has been created where large blocks of sandstone have broken away from a curved joint (a natural plane of weakness).

Halls Creek and Surrounds - **Purnululu National Park**

Around 300 million years ago, a process of mountain-building occurred. Underlying rocks in the Bungles' north and north-west – that is, the compacted gravels and sands - were uplifted and tilted. Then, over a period of 280 million years, several kilometres of overlying rock and sediment were eroded. The past 20 million years have seen a further period of uplift and have given rise to the existence of today's Bungles. The deep gorges and chasms found throughout the massif are the result of extensive water erosion along fractures joining the conglomerate and sandstone. The fractures are areas of weakness created as the pressure from overlying sedimentary rocks has been eroded away.

The beehive formations found in the north-eastern and south-western parts of the Bungles are the result of millions of years of mechanical weathering by wind, water and animals. They are extremely fragile and there appears to be no natural cement holding the sandstone particles together. It is thought that they have held together by virtue of the sand particles interlocking with one another and by the orange and black bands that help make them so distinctive.

Towering 180 metres above the chasm floor, the walls of Echidna Chasm are not more than a few metres wide for its entire 300 metre length. While sandstone is almost pure white (as evidenced by the flood-water scoured sandstone lining the chasm floor) the walls of the chasm owe their rich orange colouration to an iron-oxide coating. The boulder conglomerates contained in the walls of Echidna Chasm are thought to have been eroded by high-energy streams from glacial rocks in the Osmond Range to the north of the Bungles. They exhibit evidence of glacial scratching.

Halls Creek and Surrounds - **Purnululu National Park**

Purnululu National Park

The black bands of the beehives are made up of billions of living organisms - *Cyanobacteria* - able to survive in harsh and dry environments with limited moisture. During the northern Wet season, when far more moisture is present, the faded black colour of the Dry is replaced by a rich vibrant black colour. The orange bands are comprised of iron oxide. Despite *Cyanobacteria* constituting the black bands, the iron oxide coating represents an area of the sandstone in which there is insufficient moisture for the *Cyanobacteria* to survive.

The Bungles are home to an incredible diversity of plant and animal life, although the World-Heritage-Listing was granted as a result of the area's geological significance. During a 1992 vegetation survey, 619 species of vascular plants were recorded.[73] Thirty-five of these were of conservation significance because they were either probable new species, new records for Western Australia, new records for the Kimberley, or at the limits of their known distribution range.[74] The same survey recorded 298 species of vertebrates: including 149 birds, 41 mammals, 15 fish and 12 frogs.[75]

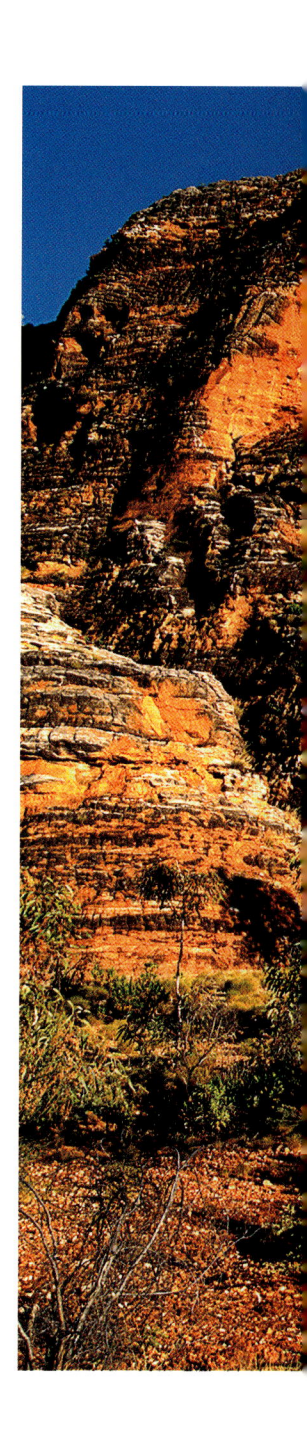

Halls Creek and Surrounds - **Purnululu National Park**

J Kununurra/Wyndham

1. Kununurra

Nestled between the immensely rugged Carr Boyd and Deception Ranges, I have come across no place in Australia that can parallel Kununurra for its proximity to such diverse and emotive scenery. The word Kununurra is a corruption of a similar-sounding Aboriginal word meaning 'Big Water'. Located on the shores of Lily Creek Lagoon, an off-shoot of Lake Kununurra, and located only kilometres from the Ord River, Kununurra was established in 1960 to service the construction of Lakes Argyle and Kununurra. Bitumen access to Kununurra was completed only in the early 1980s. Even today, and notwithstanding a major program of bridge-works in recent years to the town's south and east, the town is cut-off from the rest of Australia on an almost annual basis by Wet-season floodwaters.

Now home to a population of 6,500 people, Kununurra is the hub of a thriving agricultural industry that supports over 100 different crop varieties - including sugar-cane, mangoes, bananas, melons and sunflowers – and, with the exception of the letters "i" and "x", crops for every letter of the alphabet!

Kununurra/Wyndham - **Kununurra**

2. Lily Creek, Lake Kununurra and Sleeping Buddha

Dominated by the imposing and beautiful 'Sleeping Buddha', Lake Kununurra – or the Diversion Dam as it is otherwise known - was constructed between 1960 and 1963 as part of the first stage of the Lake Argyle Project. The Lake is 40 kilometres long and covers 165 square kilometres. It services the Ivanhoe Plains and Packsaddle Plains irrigation areas to Kununurra's north and south.

Lake Kununurra is banked up by a dam wall that is 335 metres long, 20.1 metres high and comprised of twenty 96.5 tonne gates.[76] Water to the predominantly black-soil Ivanhoe Plains is gravity fed along an irrigation channel network extending for 144 kilometres.[77] Here are many of the Ord's larger farms focusing primarily upon sugar-cane, melons and grains. Water to the Packsaddle Plains is pumped by a bank of four engines along an irrigation channel network of some 15 kilometres.[78] The entire system incorporates 160 kilometres of drains.[79]

West Packsaddle Swamp is home to more than 120 different species of birds and lies on the western part of Lake Kununurra. In 1999, and with Lake Argyle and the Ord River in between, it was added to the *Ramsar Convention* on the basis that it supports numerous rare and endangered species.

Lake Kununurra and its associated wetlands have become an important bird habitat with numbers depending upon climatic conditions throughout Australia. Dry years in Central Australia tend to result in a large migration of birds to the area. On rainy evenings during the Wet season, small turtles can be found laying eggs around the shores of the lake. Lakeview Apartments are located on the shores of Lake Kununurra and offer stunning views of Sleeping Buddha and Lily Creek.

Kununurra/Wyndham - **Lily Creek, Lake Kununurra and Sleeping Buddha**

3. Black Rock Falls

Black Rock Falls is a seasonal waterfall that plunges thirty metres over the edge of the Deception Ranges, some twenty kilometres from Kununurra. Especially after heavy monsoonal rains, the falls are visible from the Ivanhoe Road in the vicinity of the Kununurra township.

Kununurra/Wyndham - **Black Rock Falls**

4. Electrical Storm

The exact processes that give rise to lightning are still the subject of much debate. It is thought that negative ions accumulate near the bottom of the thundercloud making the bottom of the cloud negatively charged. As the cloud moves above the surface of the earth, the ground immediately below the cloud becomes positively charged (opposite charges are drawn to one another). As air is an excellent insulator, the two opposites at first cannot meet. The result is that a huge electric potential is created until such time that the air cannot hold back the negative electrons any longer. A surge of electrons rushes down to the cloud base and then on toward the ground.

The surge of electrons does not flow continuously. Rather the process occurs in a series of steps, racing down at a speed of about 220,000 kilometres per hour for 50 – 100 metres before stopping for something like one fifty millionth of a second and continuing on for another 50 – 100 metres, etc. As the electrons approach the ground, positive ions move up from the ground through protruding objects such as trees, antennae, even humans. When they meet a strong electric current moves up into the cloud along a channel a few centimetres wide. It is this return stroke that is visible to the human eye, though, its direction, due to the speed of movement is not discernable.

Because lightning is so incredibly hot – at 30,000°C it is some five times hotter than the surface of the sun – the surrounding air expands explosively. It is these shockwaves that we hear as thunder. As a general rule, for every three seconds that elapse between a lightning strike and its associated thunder, the strike is one kilometre away. However, one can still be at risk of a strike even if the storm is ten kilometres away.[80]

Without question, this was part of the most spectacular lightning show that I have seen during my time in the Kimberley. This storm forced our wait at a flood-swollen creek during our return from a wet season swim at Valentine Springs to the north of Kununurra. Earlier, dramatic, regular and close-by lightning bolts had necessitated our evacuation from the spring's warm waters.

Kununurra/Wyndham - **Electrical Storm**

5. Wyndham

Wyndham is spread out over three separate sites extending for a distance of 15 kilometres. With its Port situated at the base of the formidable Bastion Range on Cambridge Gulf, the original Port of Wyndham took hold in 1886 when it became certain that "a tremendous rush was about to set in and as a more convenient port"[81] for the Halls Creek Goldfields. During its heyday, "a great number of vessels ... arrived in the Gulf" with not less than "sixteen boats anchored in the harbour, including steamships, big sailing vessels, schooners, and steam launches" being counted on one day.[82] It is estimated that 5,000 people landed during the Halls Creek gold-rush.[83]

Today, the population of Wyndham sits at around 800 and a busy shipping schedule has been replaced with the occasional cattle and sugar transport vessels. While there are proposals for the establishment of a prawn farm a short distance away, these have stalled as parties have struggled to come to terms working with complex and impractical Native Title legislation.

Like many of the other major rivers and gulfs in northern Australia, Cambridge Gulf was named by Captain Philip Parker King during his 1819 voyage in the Mermaid in honour of His Royal Highness the Viceroy of Hanover. This voyage formed part of a quest of Australia's early European exploration to find a river that would afford access to a then thought-to-exist vast inland sea.

Wyndham was named by Sir Frederick Napier Broome, Governor of Western Australia between 1880 and 1883, after the younger son of his wife's first marriage, Major Walter George Wyndham.

Kununurra/Wyndham - **Wyndham**

Wyndham

Many of Wyndham's recent challenges can be attributed largely to the closure of the town's meatworks in 1985. From their opening in 1919, the meatworks were responsible for the slaughter of some 2,072,049 head of cattle[84] and the attraction of scores of large saltwater crocodiles to its blood-drain: the latter becoming a major tourist attraction. In 1980, Paul Flanagan, an itinerant truck-driver appears to have been taken by a saltwater crocodile while taking a late night swim upstream of the Wyndham blood-drain. His body was recovered, badly mauled but intact, from a 4 metre long male as it lay on a mudbank next to Flanagan's body: an avoidable tragedy given the prevalence of nearby warning signs.

Wyndham rates among my more favoured of the Kimberley towns both for the quality of its people and its outstanding nearby natural endowments. Few towns can boast of a more stunning vista than that atop the Bastion Lookout. There, five of the Kimberley's major rivers – the Ord, the King, the Pentecost, the Durack and the Forrest – can be seen flowing into Cambridge Gulf. On sunrise the distant fiery-orange glow of the Cockburn Range is equally emotive.

The stunning floodplains of the King River, near Wyndham, like those that line much of the expanse of Cambridge Gulf, show current-day examples of sedimentary rock being created. These floodplains are made up of muds, silts, sands and decayed plant and animal matter that have been eroded from across the Kimberley. Over the next thousands to millions of years, they will be progressively buried by more sediment. Assisted by this increasing weight and the action of fluids that are rich in silica and calcium carbonate, the buried sediment particles will one day bind together to become sedimentary rock like that found in the nearby Cockburn Range.

Kununurra/Wyndham - **Wyndham**

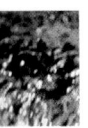

6. Crocodiles

Home to the second largest saltwater crocodile population in northern Australia – after the Northern Territory – the Kimberley is home to both the dangerous saltwater crocodile and the generally harmless freshwater crocodile. In recent years, and as a result of protection having been introduced in 1971, the saltwater crocodile population has recovered to levels where its survival now appears assured. The number of mature saltwater crocodiles in the Kimberley is estimated to be around 6,000 – 8,000.[85] The highest population densities are found in the Ord, King, Roe, Moran and Glenelg Rivers.[86] Studies of the King and Ord systems reveal a rate of natural increase approximating 2.5%[87], though no studies in the last fifteen years have covered the entire Kimberley population and none are planned.[88]

Fiction tends to get in the way of truth when discussing saltwater crocodiles. Contrary to popular belief, saltwater crocodiles are thought to prefer their food fresh. It is thought that the storage of food is the result of one or all of the crocodile's small stomach size (relative to its body mass), the fact that rotting food may attract other fresh food (eg, mud-crabs and turtles) and its slow metabolism.[89] The slow metabolism affords the crocodile short, sharp bursts of energy only that result in the build-up of lactic acid. If lactic acid builds to intolerable levels, death can result. The storage of larger prey may therefore reflect an inbuilt shut-down mechanism to avoid excess lactic acid build-up (the break-up of larger prey requires the exertion of further energy beyond the mere capture of

Saltwater crocodiles live equally well in freshwater. The highest concentrations of saltwater crocodiles in the southern hemisphere are found in the freshwater swamps and billabongs of the Arafura Swamps in the Northern Territory. For those wishing to see some of the largest saltwater crocodiles in captivity, a visit to the Wyndham Crocodile Farm is a must.

Kununurra/Wyndham - **Crocodiles**

that prey and so the crocodile stores the food to avoid exerting further energy until later). Likewise, the trapping of larger crocodiles must be approached with great care to ensure that their efforts to break capture do not prove fatal.

The majority of saltwater crocodile attacks in northern Australia have occurred during the northern Wet season. At this time of year, water temperatures more readily equate to the crocodile's optimum operating temperature: around 32 degrees. Crocodiles become more mobile and their metabolism and feeding frequency increases as higher water and air temperatures promote digestion. During the Dry season larger crocodiles, because of their large fat reserves, can live for months without feeding. It is during the warmer "build-up" and wet season months that saltwater crocodiles mate and breed.

Saltwater crocodiles larger than 5.5 metres are extremely rare. Their maximum size is generally in the range of 4.6 – 5.2 metres for males and 3.1 – 3.4 metres for females.[90]

Freshwater crocodiles are only rarely found in tidal, saline areas but can, and regularly do, co-exist with their larger saltwater cousins: particularly in the lower freshwater reaches of rivers and creeks. However, the recovery of saltwater crocodile populations – at the apparent expense of their freshwater counterparts – in areas where freshwater crocodiles had proliferated prior to the introduction of protection (freshwater crocodiles were not hunted to anywhere near the same extent) - points toward "saltie" domination in interactions between the two species.[91]

Freshwater crocodiles eat little, if anything, during the Dry and, for a given length, are slightly heavier than their saltwater counterparts: though this is somewhat deceptive given the longer tail of the saltwater crocodile.

Distinguished from saltwater crocodiles by their long, pointy snout, the normal maximum size for freshwater males is 2.0 metres and 1.8 metres for females.[92] Larger specimens frequently occur in Lake Argyle and the Ord River[93] and have been known to exceed 3.0 metres in the Northern Territory.[94]

Kununurra/Wyndham - **Crocodiles**

7. Ivanhoe Crossing

Prior to the construction of the existing concrete crossing in 1929, Ivanhoe Crossing was a sand and rock bar that afforded passage across the Ord only during the Dry season. And even then, travellers generally had to be helped across by horses, mules and/or local Aboriginal people. With the opening of the Diversion Dam bridge in 1963, the Crossing's importance as a road link has all but been removed. Previously it formed part of the main "highway" between Wyndham and the Northern Territory border. Now it remains a popular fishing spot for locals and visitors.

The areas upstream and downstream of the crossing are home to some large saltwater crocodiles, and even freshwater sharks. Despite dogs having been taken, no people have yet fallen victim in the area. Each year, numerous vehicles are lost by people misjudging the flow-rate of the river. As a general rule of thumb, vehicle crossing should not be attempted if the water is more than half-way up the pylons. A year or two back some scared individuals spent a night in a tree in the middle of the river waiting to be rescued rather than risk the perils of what lay below the surface!

The Ord River has an annual flow-rate greater than any river in Australia. In one flood, caused by cyclonic rain storms prior to construction of the Ord Dam, flow at the rate of 33,000m³ per second was recorded: enough water to fill Perth's Mundaring Wier in 38 minutes[95] and Sydney Harbour in less than 4.5 hours.[96] At 588 kilometres in length, the Ord is the Kimberley's second longest river. It drains approximately 44,000 square kilometres: an area slightly larger than the Netherlands.[97]

Kununurra/Wyndham - **Ivanhoe Crossing**

8. Lake Argyle

Located some 70 kilometres to the south of Kununurra, Lake Argyle is part of the Ord River system – the Kimberley's second longest river. Construction of the Lake Argyle Dam occurred over a 3 year period between 1969 and 1971 and the Lake filled to near capacity during the wet season of 1972/73. The area and efficiency of its catchment enables run-off from one decent wet season to easily fill the lake from empty to overflowing.

Lake Argyle, at flood storage capacity, covers an area of 2,072 square kilometres and would fill Sydney Harbour 68 times over. At normal storage levels, the Lake would fill Sydney Harbour 18 times over.[98] The average annual inflow into the Lake could meet Sydney's annual water needs for around 9 years and Perth's for approximately 17[99], though this needs to be considered in light of the fact that 25 million tonnes of sediment enter the system annually.

Lake Argyle as seen from the air. While at Lake Argyle, I undertook a cruise with Lake Argyle Tours & Cruises: a business owned and operated by the Sharpe family who have lived at the Lake since its construction. The family have an unsurpassed familiarity and knowledge of the Lake and surrounding area environs.

Kununurra/Wyndham - **Lake Argyle**

Lake Argyle

During the 1980 Wet, water levels in the lake rose by a metre in a single 24 hour period: an amount sufficient to accommodate Perth's entire water consumption at peak demand for 5 years![100] The dam wall, constructed between 1969 and 1971, is 335 metres long and 98.5 metres high[101] and, when rock-fill for the dam was blasted nearby during 1970 and 1971, the explosions set records as the biggest non-nuclear explosions in the southern hemisphere.[102]

It is estimated that the Lake is home to around 25,000 freshwater crocodiles, 30 types of fish, 237 species of bird – around 1/3 of Australia's total – and 50 types of native mammal.[103] There are between 70 and 100 sandstone and/or siltstone islands in Lake Argyle, depending upon water levels, and the Lake has been known to be home to waterspouts, winds of up to 160kmph and waves up to 3 metres.[104] During the Wet season of 1972, two people were drowned when a rain-squall capsized their cabin-cruiser.[105] Proposals are afoot to make the Lake the subject of a national park.

The Power of the Wet. Category Six rapids power down Spillway Creek, the Lake Argyle overflow, en route to the Ord River and Timor Sea.

Kununurra/Wyndham - **Lake Argyle**

9. Revolver Creek Falls

Revolver Creek is a seasonal waterfall located in the Carr Boyd Ranges to the west of Lake Argyle. It is possibly the largest single-drop Kimberley waterfall. The Carr Boyd Ranges contain some of Australia's most rugged ridges, hogbacks, cuestas and plateaux of quartz sandstone, siltstone and shale.[90] Access is only by foot or helicopter.

Kununurra/Wyndham - **Revolver Creek Falls**

10. Cockburn Range

Rising approximately 600 metres above the surrounding plains, and dominated by two linked plateaux encircled by dramatic and imposing sandstone cliffs, the Cockburn Range affords one of the most spectacular vistas in the entire Kimberley. It was discovered and named by Captain Philip Parker King - during his navigation of northern Australia from 1818 to 1820 – after Vice-Admiral Sir George Cockburn, a Lord Commissioner of the Admiralty. King was of the view that the Range so nearly resembled a "formidable fortress" that "it only wanted the display of a standard to render the illusion complete".[107]

Seen from the air, the Cockburn Range exhibits a spectacular maze of twisting and zig-zagging sandstone cliffs. With the exception of Emma Gorge, there are plans to excise the two sandstone plateaux to create a National Park when the El Questro Station lease is scheduled for renewal in 2015.

Kununurra/Wyndham - **Cockburn Range**

Cockburn Range

The Cockburn Range is made up of sedimentary rock, deposited during pre-Cambrian times, 1.8 billion years ago, and forms part of the Kimberley Plateau. The horizontal bedding of the sandstone has given the Range its flat-topped appearance. An examination of scree slopes, that characterise much of the Range's perimeter and that have been formed as rock breaks away from cliff-lines, reveals plentiful examples of ripple-rock. Ripple-rock is rock embedded with fossilised mudflat patterns and its existence suggests that the original sediments were once deposited as part of an intertidal mudflat.

Much of the Cockburn Range is bounded by scarps up to 300 metres high and the two plateaux contain a number of isolated rainforest pockets.

Kununurra/Wyndham - **Cockburn Range**

11. Ragged Range

Ragged Range is located in the East Kimberley to the west of Lake Argyle and to the north of the Argyle Diamond Mine. It is home to spectacular deep-red conglomerate domes and a number of cool refreshing gorges. The photos you see here are the result of many walks into the area and have involved significant hardship. A visit during January some years back nearly resulted in the death of my dog, Kanch, when intense heat (the temperature was well in excess of 40 degrees) and oppressive humidity (which was nearly 100%) conspired to inflict much suffering. That night remains amongst the most difficult that I have spent in the bush.

What is difficult for those that have never visited the Kimberley to understand is the effect of radiated heat, from the rock and stone that so dominate the Kimberley landscape, on one's energy levels and body. Recorded temperatures often significantly understate the true temperature out bush and one has to exercise extreme vigilance in ensuring that fluid intake is sufficient.

Failure to heed warning signs when walking in the Kimberley can prove fatal: as might have occurred during a day-walk that I undertook in September 2001. Notwithstanding that I was walking along a crystal-clear, flowing, freshwater creek, and despite having taken fluids throughout the day, my body went into shut-down mode. I stopped sweating. As I endeavoured to climb an escarpment on my way back to camp, I was halted half-way up by a feeling of extreme nausea and dizziness. Had I taken another step, there is a strong possibility that I may have died there. I slid down the escarpment's scree slope on my backside and sat in the waters of the creek for over an hour while my core body temperature cooled down.

The spectacular conglomerate domes of the Ragged Range, like the Bungle Bungles to the south, are comprised primarily of pebbles, rocks and cobbles carried by powerful streams from highlands to the east. Over time, these pebbles, rocks and cobbles were compacted, giving rise to the conglomerate that we see today, before the area was uplifted and tilted. The Ragged Range is characterised by a high escarpment and ridgeline. The "slices" in the area's unusual domes are the result of severe weathering along their many joints and fractures.

Kununurra/Wyndham - **Ragged Range**

12. Argyle Diamond Mine

The Argyle Diamond Mine is situated atop the AK1 (Argyle-Kimberlite) ore body at the head of Smoke Creek in the Ragged Range. It is the world's largest producing diamond mine and accounts for approximately 25 % of world diamond production, when measured by weight.[108] In 1994, its peak year, the mine accounted for 40% of the world's total diamond production.[109] About 5% of Argyle's production is of gem quality - including its world-renowned pink diamonds – with 25% and 70% being of industrial and near-gem quality respectively.[110] Its pink diamonds are extremely rare and make up one in every million carats of diamonds produced at the mine.[111] They are sold only by tender.

The diamonds of the AK1 pipe have been dated at 1.58 billion years and are contained within a lamproite pipe of some 2,000 metres in length and 600 metres in width at its widest point.[112] This pipe is a creation of molten rock having forced its way from 150 kilometres below the earth's surface[103] through fissures and gas-created holes that has then cooled and solidified. Its store of diamonds, constituted of pure carbon, are the result of intense heat and pressure.

Notwithstanding their reputation for being the world's hardest known substance, diamonds are brittle, and can be destroyed by a sharp blow. Similarly, and despite their ability to cut industrially in high temperature drills, they will burn and vaporise to carbon dioxide if taken to red heat. Interesting paradoxes.

At the time of its discovery, on 28 August 1979, the AK1 ore-body was incorporated within an exploration lease held by a rival uranium company. It was unclear as to whether that company intended to renew its lease when it came up for renewal and it was a tense time for the small number of CRA staff that knew of the find. As they waited to see whether the lease would be renewed, the CRA exploration team remained at Kingston's Rest, 80 kilometres to the north-west of AK1, to avoid stirring interest among rival companies.

The Argyle mine is officially projected to move into shut-down mode in 2006. Midway through 2003, Rio Tinto, the mine's owner, announced that they would shortly commence a A$70M feasibility study to assess the economic viability of taking operations underground after 2006.

Kununurra/Wyndham - **Argyle Diamond Mine**

BIBLIOGRAPHY

Agriculture Western Australia, *Ord River Irrigation Area*, Kununurra, Western Australia, 6th Edition, 1999;

Aitken, D.H., *Some Notes on Kimberley Beef Roads*, C 1969 – 1970;

Battye, J.S., *The History of the North West of Australia Embracing Kimberley, Gascoyne and Murchison Districts*, V.K. Jones & Co., Perth, 1915;

Bertram, H., Captain Bertram's Story: Naked, Hungry and Thirsty, *The West Australian*, 1932;

Bridge, P.J., *Russian Jack*, Hesperian Press, Victoria Park, 2002;

Burbidge, A.A., and McKenzie, N.L., *Wildlife Research Bulletin Number 7: The Islands of the North-west Kimberley: Western Australia*, Department of Fisheries and Wildlife, Perth, 1978;

Burbidge, A.A., McKenzie, N.L., Kenneally, K.F., *Nature Conservation Reserves in the Kimberley*, Western Australia, CALM, Perth, 1991;

Cawood, M., River of Dreams, *Australian Geographic*, July – September, Sydney, 1996;

Chalmers, C.E., and Woods, P.J., *Broome Coastal Management Plan*, Environmental Protection Authority, Perth, June 1987;

Crawford, I.M., The Benedictine Mission at Kalumburu, *Studies in Western Australian History III, Department of History*, University of Western Australia, Nedlands, 1978;

Dept. of Agriculture, *Information on Pastoral Businesses in the Rangelands of Western Australia: Edited by William Dalton and Francis Bright*, Department of Agriculture, South Perth, June 2003;

Dept. of Conservation and Land Management ("CALM"), *Kimberley Tourism Manual: A Guide to Interpreting the Kimberley for Tour Agencies, Operators, Drivers, Guides, Storytellers and Others*, CALM, Perth, 1999;

Dept. of Planning and Urban Development, *Cable Beach/ Riddell Point Broome: Development Concept Plan*, Dept. of Planning and Urban Development, Perth, 1990;

Done, C., Parks of the Plateau, *Landscape*, Perth, Autumn 2001;

Durack, P.M., Pioneering the East Kimberleys, *The Western Australian Historical Society, Journal and Proceedings*, Vol.II, 1933, Part XIV, Perth, 1933;

Edwards, H., *Kimberley: Dreaming to Diamonds*, Hugh Edwards, Perth, 1991;

Eliot, J., Birds that go to Extremes, *National Geographic*, February 2003;

Epton, K., *Rivers of the Kimberley*, Hesperian Press, Perth, 2003;

Feeken, E.H.J., Feeken, G.E.E., and Spate, O.H.K., *The Discovery and Exploration of Australia*, Thomas Nelson (Australia) Ltd, 1970;

BIBLIOGRAPHY

Forrest, A., *North-West Exploration: Journal of Expedition from De Grey to Port Darwin*, Corkwood Press, Perth, 1880;

Garrow, S., *Big Tide Country: Kimberley Tides and Tidal Life*, SC Garrow, Brighton, 2002;

Gregory, A.C., and Gregory, F.T., *Journals of Australian Explorations 1846 – 1861*, Hesperian Press, Perth, 2002;

Hale, A., New Beef Roads Recommended, *The West Australian*, 17 November 1976;

Henn, P.U., French Exploration on the Western Australian coast, *The Western Australian Historical Society, Journal and Proceedings, Vol. II, Part XV*, 1934;

Hoatson & Others, *Bungle Bungle Range: Purnululu National Park, East Kimberley, Western Australia: a Guide to the Rocks, Landforms, Plants, Animals and Human Impact*, Australian Geological Survey Organisation, Canberra, 1997;

Hordern, M., *King of the Australian Coast*, The Miegunyah Press, MUP, 1997;

Kailis, Dr P., The Passion for the Perfect Pearl: Speech conducted for the WA Business News Success and Leadership Series, Staged at the Parmelia Hilton on 11 June 2003, Published in *KAPPA: The Magazine of the MG Kailis Group*, MG Kailis Holdings Pty Ltd, Perth, 2003;

Kimberley Society, Dries, Wets & Tropical Cyclones – Weather Patterns in the Kimberley, *Boab Bulletin*, Derby, August 2002;

Kimberley Society, The Early 1960s Era in the Kimberley, *Boab Bulletin*, Derby, June 1999;

Kimberley Society, Mitchell Plateau: Past, Present and Future, *Boab Bulletin*, Derby, February 1999;

King, Captain Philip Parker, *Narrative of a Survey of the Intertropical and Western Coast of Australia, performed between the years 1818 and 1821*, Two Volumes, John Murray, London, 1827;

Lommel, A., and Lommel, K., *Rock Painting Sites in the Kimberley Region: A Description of the Paintings; An Account of an Expedition by the Staatliches Museum fur the Volkerkunde, Munich, to the North-West Australia in 1955*, Unpublished, 2003;

Lowe, P., *The Boab Tree*, Thomas C. Lothian Pty Ltd, Port Melbourne, 1998;

Lynch, J., *Wild Weather*, BBC Worldwide Limited, London, 2002;

McGregor, A., and Chester, Q., *The Kimberley: Horizons of Stone*, New Holland Publishers (Australia) Pty Ltd, 1999;

McKenzie, N., Kenneally, K. Done, C., Griffin, T., King Leopold's Treasures, *Landscope*, CALM, Perth, Autumn 1992;

Marchant, L.M., William Dampier's Significance in Australia's Maritime Discovery, T*he Royal Western Australian Historical Society, Journal and Proceedings*, pp. 43 – 61;

BIBLIOGRAPHY

Oklahoma State University Board of Regents, *Breeds of Livestock: Brahman*, Internet, 2000;

Olsen, J., Durack, M., Serventy, V., Dutton, G., *The Land Beyond Time*, Macmillan, Melbourne, 1984;

Pain, S., Flood Warnings in the Sand, *New Scientist*, 1 September 1988;

Shelmerdine, C., *El Questro: A Million Acres of Outback in the Kimberley Wilderness*, ELQ Publishing, Kununurra, 2002;

Shigley, J.E., Chapman, J., Ellison, R.K., Discovery and Mining of the Argyle Diamond Deposit, Australia, *Gems and Gemology*, Spring 2001;

Sickert, S., *Beyond the Lattice: Broome's Early Years*, Fremantle Arts Centre Press, Fremantle, 2003;

Tropical Savannas CRC, Termites, *Tropical Topics: An Interpretative Newsletter for the Tourism Industry*, No. 64, December 2000;

Tyler, I., *Geology & Landforms of the Kimberley*, CALM, Perth, 1996;

Webb, G., and Manolis, C., *Australian Crocodiles*, New Holland Publishers (Australia) Pty Ltd, Frenchs Forest, 1998;

Wildlife Management International Pty Ltd, *Final Report: Results of Spotlight and Helicopter Surveys of Crocodiles in Cambridge Gulf, Lake Argyle and Lake Kununurra*, Unpublished, 2003;

Willing, T., and Kenneally, K., *Under a Regent Moon: A Historical Account of Pioneer Pastoralists Joseph Bradshaw and Aeneas Gunn at Marigui Settlement, Prince Regent River, Kimberley, Western Australia, 1891 – 1892*, CALM, Perth, 2002;

Woldendorp, R., Australia: *The Untamed Land*, Reader's Digest (Australia) Pty Ltd, 1995.

Zell, L., *A Guide to the Kimberley Coast Wilderness – North Western Australia*, Wild Discovery, 2003 at pp. 61 – 2.

FOOTNOTES

[1] Quoting Grey, G., *Journals of Two Expeditions of Discovery in North-west and Western Australia during the years 1837, 38 and 39*, Hesperian Press, 1984 at p.216.

[2] Durack, MG, *The Western Australian Historical Society, Journal and Proceedings*, Quoting Stokes LJ in An Outline of North Australian History, From Cambridge Gulf to the Victoria River, Vol II, 1932, Part XII at p.3.

[3] Quoted in Bain, M., *Full Fathom Five*, Artlook Books, Perth, 1982 at p.227.

[4] Sickert, S., *Beyond the Lattice: Broome's Early Years*, Fremantle Arts Centre Press, Fremantle, 2003.

[5] Refer Dept. of Planning and Urban Development, *Cable Beach/ Riddell Point Broome: Development Concept Plan*, Dept. of Planning and Urban Development, Perth, 1990 and Chalmers, C.E., and Woods, P.J., *Broome Coastal Management Plan*, Environmental Protection Authority, Perth, June 1987. These reports give an excellent analysis of the coastal processes occurring around Broome.

[6] Chalmers, C.E., and Woods, P.J., *Broome Coastal Management Plan*, Environmental Protection Authority, Perth, June 1987 at p. 27.

[7] Marchant, L.M., William Dampier's Significance in Australia's Maritime Discovery, T*he Royal Western Australian Historical Society, Journal and Proceedings*, pp. 43 – 61.

[8] These figures were initially taken from a speech given by Glen Cook of the Bureau of Meteorology in Perth to the Kimberley Society on 7 August 2002. Independent analysis of Kimberley weather data was undertaken by the author to corroborate the information outlined in the speech of Mr Cook.

[9] Chalmers, C.E., and Woods, P.J., *Broome Coastal Management Plan*, Environmental Protection Authority, Perth, June 1987 at p.31.

[10] Willing, T., and Kenneally, K., *Under a Regent Moon: A historical account of pioneer pastoralists Joseph Bradshaw and Aeneas Gunn at Marigui Settlement, Prince Regent River, Kimberley, Western Australia, 1891 – 1892*, CALM, Perth, 2002., at pp 35 – 36.

[11] Henn, P.U., French Exploration on the Western Australian coast, *The Western Australian Historical Society, Journal and Proceedings, Vol. II, Part XV*, 1934 at p.17.

[12] Hordern, M., *King of the Australian Coast*, The Miegunyah Press, MUP, 1997 at.p.312.

[13] Chalmers, C.E., and Woods, P.J., *Broome Coastal Management Plan*, Environmental Protection Authority, Perth, June 1987 at pp. 12 – 13.

[14] Chalmers, C.E., and Woods, P.J., *Broome Coastal Management Plan*, Environmental Protection Authority, Perth, June 1987 at p.17.

[15] Battye, J.S., *The History of the North West of Australia Embracing Kimberley, Gascoyne and Murchison Districts*, V.K. Jones & Co., Perth, 1915 at p.4.

[16] Dampier's 1688 landing site is uncertain. His journals or field notes have not been located by researchers and one can only work on two general accounts which were written some time after his voyage had finished; the first being his book the New Voyage Around the World; and, a shorter manuscript in Sloan Manuscript 3236 in the British Library. What complicates matters further is that these two accounts differ markedly. If the former version is correct then one must look to his likely landing spot as being on the Dampier Peninsula that could be anywhere from Beagle Bay on the western side of the Peninsula to Swan Point to the east of Cape Leveque. If the latter account is to be accepted, then one must look to the Joseph Bonaparte Gulf to the east of Cambridge Gulf as being the likely landing spot. A strong analysis of this matter is outlined in Marchant, L.M., William Dampier's Significance in Australia's Maritime Discovery, *The Royal Western Australian Historical Society, Journal and Proceedings*, pp. 43 – 61.

[17] Refer Marchant, L.M., William Dampier's Significance in Australia's Maritime Discovery, T*he Royal Western Australian Historical Society, Journal and Proceedings,*, pp. 43 – 61. Contrary to popular belief, it would appear that Dampier did not land at Roebuck Bay and that the bay he referred to was in fact Lagrange Bay at the northern end of the Eighty Mile Beach.

[18] Henn, P.U., French Exploration on the Western Australian coast, *The Western Australian Historical Society, Journal and Proceedings, Vol. II, Part XV*, 1934 at pp. 12 and 17.

[19] Portions of the Coast are currently protected as Marine Parks, Conservation Reserves and National Parks, but much of it remains unprotected.

[20] Burbidge, A.A., McKenzie, N.L., Kenneally, K.F., *Nature Conservation Reserves in the Kimberley*, Western Australia, CALM, Perth, 1991 at p.iii.

[21] Zell, L., *A Guide to the Kimberley Coast Wilderness – North Western Australia*, Wild Discovery, 2003 at pp. 61 – 2.

FOOTNOTES

[22] Sickert, S., *Beyond the Lattice: Broome's Early Years*, Fremantle Arts Centre Press, Fremantle, 2003 at p.24.

[23] Kailis, Dr P., The Passion for the Perfect Pearl: Speech conducted for the WA Business News Success and Leadership Series, Staged at the Parmelia Hilton on 11 June 2003, Published in *KAPPA: The Magazine of the MG Kailis Group*, MG Kailis Holdings Pty Ltd, Perth, 2003.

[24] Ibid.

[25] Sickert, S., *Beyond the Lattice: Broome's Early Years*, Fremantle Arts Centre Press, Fremantle, 2003 at p.42.

[26] Kailis, Dr P., The Passion for the Perfect Pearl: Speech conducted for the WA Business News Success and Leadership Series, Staged at the Parmelia Hilton on 11 June 2003, Published in *KAPPA: The Magazine of the MG Kailis Group*, MG Kailis Holdings Pty Ltd, Perth, 2003.

[27] Garrow, S., *Big Tide Country: Kimberley Tides and Tidal Life*, SC Garrow, Brighton, 2002 at p.33.

[28] Ibid.

[29] Bertram, H., Captain Bertram's Story: Naked, Hungry and Thirsty, *The West Australian*, 1932.

[30] Ibid. This personal account gives an excellent and authentic first-hand understanding of the aviators' incredible survival story.

[31] Epton, K., *Rivers of the Kimberley*, Hesperian Press, Perth, 2003 at p.30.

[32] Dept. of Conservation and Land Management, *Kimberley Tourism Manual: A Guide to Interpreting the Kimberley for Tour Agencies, Operators, Drivers, Guides, Storytellers and Others*, CALM, Perth, 1999 at p.2.1.22.

[33] King, Captain Philip Parker, Narrative of a Survey of the Intertropical and Western Coast of Australia, performed between the years 1818 and 1821, Two Volumes, John Murray, London, 1827 at p.88.

[34] Feeken, E.H.J., Feeken, G.E.E., and Spate, O.H.K., *The Discovery and Exploration of Australia*, Thomas Nelson (Australia) Ltd, 1970.

[35] Epton, K., *Rivers of the Kimberley*, Hesperian Press, Perth, 2003 at p.21.

[36] Ibid.

[37] Dept. of Agriculture, *Information on Pastoral Businesses in the Rangelands of Western Australia: Edited by William Dalton and Francis Bright*, Department of Agriculture, South Perth, June 2003 at p.5.

[38] Oklahoma State University Board of Regents, *Breeds of Livestock: Brahman*, Internet, 2000.

[39] Shelmerdine, C., *El Questro: A Million Acres of Outback in the Kimberley Wilderness*, ELQ Publishing, Kununurra, 2002 at p.37 and p.42.

[40] Ibid at p.24.

[41] Crawford, I.M., The Benedictine Mission at Kalumburu, *Studies in Western Australian History III, Department of History*, University of Western Australia, Nedlands, 1978, p.44.

[42] Done, C., *Parks of the Plateau*, Landscape, Perth, Autumn 2001 at p.52;

[43] Burbidge, A.A., McKenzie, N.L., Kenneally, K.F., *Nature Conservation Reserves in the Kimberley*, Western Australia, CALM, Perth, 1991 at p.71;

[44] Refer to a speech given by Ron Johnstone and recorded at the following source: Kimberley Society, Mitchell Plateau: Past, Present and Future, *Boab Bulletin*, Derby, February 1999;

[45] Epton, K., *Rivers of the Kimberley*, Hesperian Press, Perth, 2003 at p.43.

[46] Done, C., *Parks of the Plateau*, Landscape, Perth, Autumn 2001 at p.50.

[47] Lommel, A., and Lommel, K., *Rock Painting Sites in the Kimberley Region: A Description of the Paintings; An Account of an Expedition by the Staatliches Museum fur die Volkerkunde, Munich, to the North-West Australia in 1955*, Unpublished, 2003. This excellent, as-yet unpublished account can be viewed on the Bradshaw Foundation website at www.bradshawfoundation.com. Whether it will ever be published will be a matter for the Western Australian Museum and Department of Indigenous Affairs to decide.

[48] Based on telephone interviews with the direct and immediate descendents of pioneers that settled the Gibb River and Manning Gorge area.

FOOTNOTES

[49] Epton, K., *Rivers of the Kimberley*, Hesperian Press, Perth, 2003 at p.2.

[50] Based on telephone interviews with former managers of Mt Barnett Station.

[51] Forrest, A., *North-West Exploration: Journal of Expedition from De Grey to Port Darwin*, Perth, 1880 at p.19;

[52] Epton, K., *Rivers of the Kimberley*, Hesperian Press, Perth, 2003 at p.32.

[53] Lowe, P., *The Boab Tree*, Thomas C. Lothian Pty Ltd, Port Melbourne, 1998, p. 46. This book is an excellent resource for those wishing to learn more about the Boab tree.

[54] Ibid at p.48

[55] Ibid.

[56] Ibid at p.49.

[57] Kimberley Society, The Early 1960s Era in the Kimberley, *Boab Bulletin*, Derby, June 1999.

[58] Quoted in Edwards, H., *Kimberley: Dreaming to Diamonds*, Hugh Edwards, Perth, 1991 at p.33. Note, the words "reported to have said" are used in the text to reflect the fact that Edwards does not footnote his references nor provide a Bibliography.

[59] Dept. of Conservation and Land Management ("CALM"), *Kimberley Tourism Manual: A Guide to Interpreting the Kimberley for Tour Agencies, Operators, Drivers, Guides, Storytellers and Others*, CALM, Perth, 1999 at p.4.6.1.

[60] Epton, K., *Rivers of the Kimberley*, Hesperian Press, Perth, 2003.

[61] As outlined in my text, the reef system extends for 350 kilometres: significantly more than the 40 miles (64 kilometres) referred to by Camp.

[62] Olsen, J., Durack, M., Serventy, V., Dutton, G., *The Land Beyond Time*, Macmillan, Melbourne, 1984.

[63] Edwards, H., *Kimberley: Dreaming to Diamonds*, Hugh Edwards, Perth, 1991 at p.109.

[64] Pain, S., Flood Warnings in the Sand, *New Scientist*, 1 September 1988;

[65] Lynch, J., *Wild Weather*, BBC Worldwide Limited, London, 2002.

[66] Bridge, P.J., *Russian Jack*, Hesperian Press, Victoria Park, 2002 at p.30.

[67] Ibid at p.2

[68] Boab Bulletin, *Wolfe Creek Meteorite Crater*, April 1997. This article details a speech given by Dr Alex Bevan to the Kimberley Society on 3 April 1997.

[69] Department of Conservation and Land Management ("CALM"), Kimberley Tourism Manual: A Guide to Interpreting the Kimberley for Tour Agencies, Operators, Drivers, Guides, Storytellers and Others, CALM, Perth, 1999 at p.2.3.34.

[70] Burbidge, A.A., and McKenzie, N.L., *Wildlife Research Bulletin Number 7: The Islands of the North-west Kimberley: Western Australia*, Department of Fisheries and Wildlife, Perth, 1978 at p.100.

[71] Gregory, A.C. and Gregory, F.T., Journal of the North Australian Exploring Expedition, by A.C., Gregory in *Journals of Australian Exploration 1846 - 1861*, Hesperian Press, Perth, 2002 at p.138.

[72] Tropical Savannas CRC, Termites, *Tropical Topics: An Interpretative Newsletter for the Tourism Industry*, No. 64, December 2000.

[73] Hoatson & Others, Bungle Bungle Range: Purnululu National Park, East Kimberley, Western Australia: a Guide to the Rocks, Landforms, Plants, Animals and Human Impact, Australian Geological Survey Organisation, Canberra, 1997 at p.23. This book gives an excellent overview of the geology, history and flora and fauna of the Bungles and surrounding areas.

[74] Ibid.

[75] Ibid at p.28.

[76] Agriculture Western Australia, Ord River Irrigation Area, Kununurra, Western Australia, 6th Edition, 1999.

[77] Sourced from telephone interviews with the Ord Irrigation Cooperative.

[78] Ibid.

FOOTNOTES

[79] Ibid.

[80] Lynch, J., *Wild Weather*, BBC Worldwide Limited, London, 2002. An excellent lay discussion of the processes giving rise to thunder and lightening, and the weather more generally is contained in this very readable, interesting and enjoyable book.

[81] Durack, P.M., Pioneering the East Kimberleys, *The Western Australian Historical Society, Journal and Proceedings*, Vol.II, 1933, Part XIV, Perth, 1933 at p.37.

[82] Ibid at p.39.

[83] Ibid.

[84] Based on telephone interview with Wyndham Historical Society member, Viv McMicking.

[85] A number of people with expertise in undertaking crocodile surveys were spoken to about the likely mature crocodile population in the Kimberley. The figure used was taken from Russell Gueho who participated in numerous crocodile surveys while working as a wildlife officer in Kununurra.

[86] Ibid.

[87] Wildlife Management International Pty Ltd, *Final Report: Results of Spotlight and Helicopter Surveys of Crocodiles in Cambridge Gulf, Lake Argyle and Lake Kununurra*, 2003, Report commissioned by CALM at p.12

[88] Based on telephone interview with Dr Peter Mawson, the CALM person charged with monitoring of crocodile populations.

[89] Webb, G., and Manolis, C., *Australian Crocodiles: A Natural History*, New Holland Publishers (Australia) Pty Ltd, Frenchs Forest, 1998 at p.72.

[90] Ibid at p.65.

[91] Ibid at p.53.

[92] Ibid at p.95

[93] Based on discussions with Russell Gueho, a former Kununurra-based CALM wildlife officer now living in Broome.

[94] Ibid at p.95.

[95] Epton, K., *Rivers of the Kimberley*, Hesperian Press, Perth, 2003 at p.48.

[96] Cawood, M., River of Dreams, *Australian Geographic*, July – September, 1996, pp.69-91.

[97] Epton, K., *Rivers of the Kimberley*, Hesperian Press, Perth, 2003 at p.48.

[98] Based on information supplied from the Water and Rivers Commission. Lake Argyle, at flood storage volume, holds 34,655 Gigalitres of water. Sydney Harbour holds 504 Gigalitres of water. 34,655/504 therefore equals 68.76.

[99] Ibid.

[100] Cawood, M., River of Dreams, *Australian Geographic*, July – September, 1996, pp.69-91.

[101] Ibid.

[102] Ibid at p.73.

[103] Ibid at p. 72 and fold-out.

[104] Ibid and also discussions with Charlie Sharpe of Lake Argyle Cruises.

[105] Ibid at p.72.

[106] Burbidge, A.A., McKenzie, N.L., Kenneally, K.F., *Nature Conservation Reserves in the Kimberley*, Western Australia, CALM, Perth, 1991 at p.35.

[107] Hordern, M., *King of the Australian Coast*, The Miegunyah Press, MUP, 1997 at.p.200.

[108] Shigley, J.E., Chapman, J., Ellison, R.K., Discovery and Mining of the Argyle Diamond Deposit, Australia, *Gems and Gemology*, Spring 2001 at p.26.

[109] Ibid.

[110] Ibid at p.37.

[111] Ibid at p.

[112] Ibid at p.31.

[113] Ibid at p.40